FROM BLURRY TO BRILLIANT

ERIC MINA

This book is dedicated to two men who shaped my life in countless ways with their love and patience.

The first is my father who has been there for me my whole life. Dad, you did the job of two parents. Because of you, my brother and I never went without anything – least of all love and attention. You've shown me exactly the kind of person and father I want to be.

The second is my uncle Eddie. Not only did you push me to write this book, but you've always believed in the potential of my weirdness. You helped me to push myself and stretch my boundaries every day. Thank you.

I love you both so much. Thanks for all you did. This book wouldn't have been possible without you.

Foreword

For roughly three decades I've been teaching students, salespeople, and business leaders that the key to personal achievement is focus. If you can train your mind to zero in on a singular goal you can make amazing things happen.

That lesson has never been as important as it is today. On one side of our lives, there are new pressures and competitors everywhere. And on the other side, we have so many more distractions than we used to. It's getting hard to pay attention to what matters, but the rewards for tuning out the noise all around you make it worth it to set the right habits.

The book you're reading right now can help. When I first met Eric, I had an immediate sense that he could help teach a new generation of students and professionals about the power of concentration. He didn't just have a unique story and a strong sense of humor, but also a passion for helping others to see past their own self-imposed limitations. He had figured out what it meant to break free from invisible barriers and wanted others to find that strength in themselves.

Since then I've been impressed with his ideas and the gift he has for expressing them. Whether it's in writing or during a seminar, he can take the best pieces of insight from dozens of sources and weave them together in a way that's both informative and entertaining. He can show you how to get moving in your life or career without getting bogged down in the minutia.

It would be hard to come up with a better example of mental self-mastery than a person who has overcome ADHD to succeed as a coach, speaker, hypnotist and author. The lessons he picked up set him on a completely different course than the one he seemed to be born with. They can do the same for you.

I hope you'll keep that in mind as you move through this book. When I first read it, I found it to be fast and entertaining. It's also deceptively informative. Enjoy the stories, but also remember that with just a small bit of effort and intention you can find new levels of success, too.

Wherever you are right now, and whatever you're going through (good or bad), I'm sure you have goals you want to reach. What you're about to find is a set of proven ideas and principles that can help bring you closer to them. I suggest you read them carefully, and then re-read them if necessary. Do what it takes to make them a part of your life. Your subconscious mind is a powerful thing, and this is the foreword to your owner's manual.

I'm proud to be able to introduce you to this book

and its author. My hope is that all the adventure and success Eric has found will come to you, too. You're capable of amazing things. Read on and learn how to focus on them.

Anthony Galie

Motivational speaker and author of *Take Control of Your Subconscious Mind*

Introduction

Can We Focus on What Matters for a Minute?

We all wish we had more time. Many of us wish for more energy, or more motivation. Almost everyone you'll ever meet has a desire for more money. What we tend to be lacking more than anything, however, is the one thing that could help us get all of these: *the ability to focus*.

Collectively, we have too many distractions. When so many things are demanding our attention, it

stops us from being as productive as we should be and holds us back from our dreams.

Look around and you'll see we are living in a constantly distracted state. We are on our phones while sitting behind the wheel and walking through busy intersections. We are streaming shows and listening to podcasts while we're supposed to study. We are missing important details in classes and meetings because we can't ignore text messages.

More importantly, we are allowing ourselves to be interrupted by what's right in front of us rather than focusing on what actually matters in our lives.

It might just seem like a symptom of our modern age, but distraction doesn't have to be a way of life. I should know – not only do I have to fight the same urges as everyone else, but I have been doing so (medication-free) for all of my adult life while battling ADHD. My brain simply isn't wired to stay on track.

I realized a long time ago that a tendency to shift attention from one topic or inspiration to another was never going to help me get ahead. So, I started looking for ways to train myself to focus. What I found along the way wasn't just a blueprint for keeping my brain on track, but also a way of living that lends itself to goal achievement and even my own happiness.

In this book, I'm going to share my seven secrets for maintaining focus. I'm going to give you usable tips that won't just help you concentrate at a given moment, but also throughout your life. So, if you have a tendency to give up when you should be studying or working on a business project, for example, my lessons should give you some instant relief. At the same time, I want you to walk away with a concrete set of ideas you can use to stay focused on your bigger goals, too.

In my mind, both halves of this equation are important. A big part of maintaining your concentration is simply being "locked in" on what's in front of you when it's important to do so. However, distracted living isn't just about the moment-to-moment mental drift most of us are so familiar with. It can also stop you from achieving the life you've been working towards because some other minor inspiration or priority is always ready to jump in the way.

If that all sounds familiar to you, read on. But before you do I'm going to make a promise: this won't be a book filled with dry concepts and theories. While I will give you the occasional quote or factoid, most of what I'm going to share will come in the form of personal experiences and first-person advice. In other words, I'm going to tell you all the different ways I got life wrong, what I learned from it, and how you can do better.

Learning how to focus my mind and actions has literally transformed my way of thinking. It has taken me from blurry to brilliant. If that's possible for someone like me, who has a brain that is wired for constant stimulus and distraction, just imagine what these tips can do for you.

Once upon a time, I thought my life was going nowhere. But, I soon learned that a person who can stay concentrated on what they want to achieve always has a huge advantage over the rest of the pack. No matter where you're starting from, or what you want to achieve, I absolutely believe that maintaining focus will be one of the big keys to moving forward and creating momentum.

So, if you're ready to take the next step, and hear about a few of my crazy stories along the way, turn the page and let's get started!

ONE

You Shouldn't Listen to Me (But Do It Anyway)

"Dude, why are you flirting with my Grandmother?"

This was an actual question asked to me by a friend many years ago. I was in high school at the time, and had been invited over to his house for dinner. After the meal, I had a great conversation with his grandma, absorbing seven decades' worth of stories. At some point he apparently felt I had crossed a line.

Until my friend spoke up, though, I wasn't aware I was doing anything strange. After all, his grandmother was a fascinating person, but I wasn't actually *that* attracted to her (just kidding). I simply liked hearing about what she had seen in the world. His question made me feel a little self-conscious. At first I wondered whether I had done something wrong. Then I got curious: was his gammy trying to flirt with me?

It might seem strange to start a book on focus with such an awkward moment from my teenage years, but I think it's the perfect starting point for the journey we're about to dive into together for two reasons. First, because I want you to know right off the bat that I can be a little bit of a strange guy. It took me a long time to come to grips with it, but I guess I'm just not quite like most other people. I'm curious about a great deal of what I hear and see, and I'm not really afraid of looking silly if it means I can learn something interesting.

The second thing I want you to know is that I've always been fascinated by people. I love finding out about what they think, how their perspectives have been shaped, and the underlying feelings or motivations that drive them. It's that keen interest that drove me to study psychology, to become a hypnotist performing across North America, and even to research and write this book.

I'm getting ahead of myself, though. What really matters is that I'm a student of the human mind, both in the formal and informal sense. I learned very early on that my brain doesn't quite work the way most other peoples' brains do, but that we are all facing similar sets of challenges and obstacles when it comes to bringing our best selves to life. Each of us is unique, but we face the same obstacles to happiness and success.

This book is going to give you a little bit of my slightly-odd story. More than that, it's going to offer some solid advice you can use right now. I don't mean theory, or big ideas that sound great on a social media post but aren't useful when you actually try them; I'm talking real-world tips you can use to be happier and more successful. Finally, we're going to have a little fun along the way.

If that all sounds good to you, let's dive in…

I'm the Luxury Import You Didn't Know You Wanted

Since I'm usually traveling between shows and speeches each week, I have plenty of time to watch movies. One thing you notice, when you watch as many films as I do, is that a lot of the big screen heroes – even the ones who are based on real people – seem as if they were always destined for greatness. They've always been the biggest, the fastest, or the wittiest. It feels only natural when they end up saving the day.

Once in a while, though, the writers and directors give us a hero who has to work a little to find their hidden talents or special powers. I always like those movies best. That's probably because my own start to life didn't suggest I would turn out to be anything special. Certainly, most of the adults who knew me as a child probably never suspected I could become an author, speaker, and public figure.

To understand why I did, and why it matters to you in your search for focus and achievement, we have to go all the way back to the beginning.

I come from Pennsylvania, but if you've met me or glanced at my author photo you can probably guess my whole family didn't arrive on a wooden boat from Europe in the 16th century. My dad came to America when he was 9 years old. He integrated fully into his new country, even fighting for the U.S. in Vietnam.

Both my parents worked in hospitals. After they met

and married, they decided to work overseas in Saudi Arabia as a way to earn extra money while getting their new family started. During the five years they spent in the Middle East my brother and I were born.

During a family vacation, we spent a few days in Austria. It was there that my mother was killed in a traffic accident while protecting me. Even though I can't remember much about her from my own direct impressions, her love, sacrifice, and loss have stayed with me every day since.

People occasionally ask me if it's difficult to be an immigrant. The most honest answer I can give them is: "How would I know?" I was born as a U.S. citizen and can't remember anything before my time on the East coast. If anything, I like to consider myself a luxury import.

My dad had been a nuclear medical technician overseas, but as a new widower and single father of two, he didn't want to spend long hours working at a hospital. So rather than returning to his old line of work, he gathered together whatever savings he could find and bought a small video store. Even in a closer setting he couldn't keep a close eye on us for every waking hour, so he would let my brother and I watch movies. In that way, Hollywood babysat us on and off for years, keeping us occupied with tales of ninja turtles and courageous soldiers.

I always knew and understood from an early age that movies weren't real. They were simply made up stories. Still, I found them absolutely absorbing. Even though my brother would eventually get bored marathon film session, I could stay locked into the onscreen stories for hours at a time. What I didn't know then was that my brain was wired just a bit differently than his, and from the way most other people's minds work too.

Why the Best Advice on Focus Comes from the Worst Person to Teach it

As a kid, I had no idea what ADHD meant. I just knew I always seemed to be in trouble for something.

At home, I was always active. If I wasn't watching a movie, I was running from one room to another, imagining life-or-death scenarios where only a dashing hero (myself, of course) could come to the rescue. Adults were always reminding me to sit still, but it never had any effect.

If we went somewhere public, like a restaurant, my father would quickly become stressed. It wasn't just that I wouldn't remain calmly in a seat or a booth. Before we could even get our food I would be running around the restaurant, diving under other tables, or chatting up the waitstaff.

I wasn't just curious, I was *over*-curious. That was fine when I was engrossed in games, puzzles, or films. It was tougher to deal with when I was breaking merchandise in stores or taking apart household items to see how they worked. My interest in all things wasn't improved by my clumsiness. My dad was always worried I was going to bust whatever I picked up. He was right – I usually did.

On one particularly energetic outing, my father took me to a Little League baseball game. It was the summer before first grade, and my brother was playing. Instead of watching him compete, or playing quietly, I was running around like a wild animal behind the bleachers, ignoring my dad's pleas to come and sit with him.

In the midst of this chaos, another parent noticed my behavior and decided to have a word with my dad. She mentioned that she'd had similar problems with her own son, and that the right medication could make a big difference. My father had been very resistant to the idea of putting me on any pills. At the same time, years of frustration and persistent worries about my future eventually swayed him to consider the idea. A business card was shared and an appointment was made. It didn't take long for the psychologist to diagnose me with a strong case of ADHD, and after some back-and-forth with my dad, a prescription was written.

The pills helped, a little, but I still struggled to concentrate on things that didn't interest me. Even worse, there were some side effects. For instance, I rarely slept more than five or six hours per night. I would stay up past midnight watching television with my dad (M.A.S.H. was my favorite), and then be up well before I needed to for school. The result gave me some odd personality twists. It was like I was a regular child who just happened to be pulling all-night shifts as a security guard.

The bigger effect, though, was that my mind felt

dulled. The world was simply a little bit less vivid than it had been before. My energy, and my emotions, were all turned down like the volume on television. In some ways, that was probably a good thing. My grades improved, and some of the behaviors that most aggravated my father went away. At the same time, though, I realized I just didn't feel like myself anymore.

The contrast was especially noticeable when I would go off of my medication for short periods of time. For a while, my father didn't realize I had to take my pills every day. So, I would be away from school for a weekend and go cold turkey. By Saturday morning I would begin to feel like my normal, happy, and energized self again.

Those unmedicated days felt wonderful to me, but adults could easily tell the difference. I can vividly remember one of my friend's moms asking me not to come play if I hadn't taken my pills. It was just too much for her to deal with. Experiences like those taught me there was one version of myself the world expected, and a different one that made me feel happy. The tug-of-war between the two kept growing and growing through elementary and middle school.

That sensation got to be harder and harder to live with. Eventually, I realized I needed to make some important changes for myself.

Exploring the Owner's Manual for My Mind

Once I reached eighth grade, I realized I couldn't keep being two different people. Even though the pills I took were turning me into a version of myself that a lot of people preferred, I couldn't imagine living most of my waking life in a blur. So, I decided to stop taking my ADHD medication.

This was a decision that didn't go over as well as I might have hoped.

My father was torn. On the one hand, he was way ahead of his time when it came to things like organics, the dangers of unknown chemicals, and the value of fresh fruit and vegetables. He wouldn't let us drink diet soda, so the idea of pumping me full of psychoactive drugs wasn't his favorite notion ever.

On the other hand, he took the news that I wanted to stop taking the medication that made it possible for me to succeed in school with something between fear and fury. He knew I wasn't completely happy, but he also saw from the outside that things were going well. He felt the way so many parents would – that my good grades would lead to success and a happy life. How, he asked me, would I get along without my medication? How could I expect to succeed if I couldn't concentrate for more than ten seconds at a time?

My only answer was that I'd have to figure it out. I knew I needed to learn to live without a pharmaceutical crutch, and he eventually agreed to let me at least try.

Initially, it seemed as if things weren't going to work out. My attention wandered during school and my grades began to suffer. A's and B's turned to C's and D's. It seemed as if the future my dad hoped I could achieve, the one where I would maybe become a doctor or a lawyer, was slipping out of reach.

In the midst of it all, though, I was happier than I had been in a long time. I started feeling like myself again, and my mind looked for solutions now that it was free to roam. That was when one of the first turning points in my young academic life arrived. A teacher noticed I was constantly struggling with attention. As it turned out, her husband had also spent a lifetime wrestling with ADHD, and she passed along a book he had found very helpful.

The book was titled *Attention Deficit Hyperactive Disorder: A New Perspective* by Thom Hartmann. It changed my life. The author didn't view my condition as a handicap; instead, he thought of it as a different type of brain wiring that happened to be more beneficial in some environments than others. His hypothesis was that ADHD was really a hunter's mindset. When searching for prey, the hunter has to see and react to multiple different things at once. They are drawn into the stimulus, using it for clues about their environment and next steps. A hunter doesn't just *want* to see everything at once, he *has* to.

The problem for individuals with ADHD, he pointed out, was that we were living in a farmer's world. Our society rewards slow, methodical thinking, rather than rapid impulses and quick action. Kids like me often did well at sports, or in certain subjects, but we hated the drier aspects of life at school. That certainly spoke to me. There was a certain irony in realizing I had to read a book to understand why I had always hated reading books.

That one set of ideas changed my entire outlook and

perspective. I came to realize there wasn't anything about my mind that was holding me back. Instead, I just had to use my gifts a little differently while making up for my weaknesses the same way everyone else does.

I would love to say that this realization changed my academic performance overnight, but the truth is I still struggled to concentrate and remained a solid C student throughout my high school years. However, that little breakthrough was enough for me to start looking for more information and answers. Despite my low GPA, and years of lectures from teachers about how I probably wouldn't amount to much, I was determined to earn a degree.

I applied to Keystone College, which was close to home, and barely got accepted. I had to spend a year under academic probation. I didn't care. I was in and that was all that mattered. My grades weren't spectacular, but good enough to allow me to eventually transfer to Penn State. That's when things really started to take off for me.

Fixing Your Mind is Fixing Your Life

Sometimes, things that seem inevitable to you later in life feel like small strokes of luck in the moment. During my time at PSU I served on the student committee for entertainment. As part of our scheduling for the semester we brought in a magician and mentalist for a show one evening.

I was mesmerized by what I saw. The tricks and illusions he showed off were even more entrancing than the films I had grown to love so much over the years. The performer, a great guy by the name of Wayne Hoffman was kind enough to give me some of his time and insight as I buried him under an avalanche of questions. My over-curious mind threw ideas at him until he finally pointed me towards a book I could check out to learn some magic tricks. He even gave me some advice on how I could get started putting together a routine of my own.

With that little bit of encouragement, I was off to the races. I practiced a handful of card tricks and illusions again and again for half a year until I could pull them off convincingly. Before long I was getting booked to do small local appearances for extra money. I saw Wayne again when he returned to PSU the next year. I was proud to show him how far I'd come. It was then he made a suggestion that would change my life: that I look into hypnotism.

I was already excited about the options in front of me and took his advice immediately. I was referred to the National Guild of Hypnotists and discovered they had a course coming up in my area.

I learned more in my single week of training with their instructors than I did in a four-year college psychology program. That isn't a knock on higher education, just a recognition that hypnosis is more concrete and actionable than the theories you pick up in a textbook. I was having a lot of fun putting people into a trance state, but more importantly I was learning new ways I could help others.

Somewhere along the way, I figured out you can

actually use the power of the subconscious mind to change someone's core thinking, beliefs, and habits. You can help them move on from pain or limiting ideas, switching their internal perspectives to something more positive. You can actually improve their lives just by helping them to find the tools that are already inside of them.

I also discovered some of the keys to helping myself and finding lasting success. After all, hypnotism is really all about focus and intent. Once you break through the entertaining routines and rituals, hypnotizing someone is really just putting them in a calm and concentrated state.

In the years since, I have seen and demonstrated the power of a focused mind again and again. I've had the chance to share some valuable lessons, and more than a few laughs, with thousands of people. What I never got the opportunity to do, though, was show the students and business people I work with how to harness the power of their own concentration. This book is my guide to not only bring clarity to your mind, but also using that clarity to reach whatever personal or professional goals matter most to you.

If this were a movie, I would be a very unlikely hero. I didn't get a fantastic start to life, and I sometimes think I might be the worst person in the world to teach others about focus. At the same time, though, I was told again and again that I wouldn't be successful. Teachers reminded me I could never be a doctor or a lawyer. More than one psychologist suggested I might be beyond help.

Today, I live a fantastic life. I've been more successful than my father and brother ever thought I could be. All the good things that have come my way have been a result of my single-minded focus on reaching the right goals. If the lessons I've picked up can help me, then I know they can do wonders for you, too.

TWO

The Power of Focus in an ADHD World

In the movies, the hero comes to a stunning realization, or a moment of clarity, and immediately sets off in a new direction. Armed with a new sense of resolve and determination, he or she takes their problems head-on and fights every obstacle to succeed.

While I will continue to insist that I *am* the hero in this book, I'm sad to say that just deciding to overcome my attention deficit issues didn't fix anything. In fact, I was a bit of a mess at first. I think it took about five minutes for most of my friends and teachers to realize when I'd gone off my medication. While my senses weren't being dulled anymore, to the outside world I seemed like a small child. I just couldn't be calm or stop the flood of ideas constantly coursing through my mind.

Sitting in a classroom became a struggle. I didn't want to stay still, and I would have trouble concentrating on what my teachers were saying. Being off Ritalin cured me of my shyness, but it meant I wanted to talk to *everyone*. I had plenty to say, whether it was on-topic or not. I might have been socially awkward, but I sure didn't feel it.

In the lunchroom, I would sit with my friends and discuss five different topics over the course of just a few minutes. That might have been interesting, except I was having the conversations largely by myself. It was like I was having a verbal tennis match with my own brain. The people around me were just spectators. The ideas would just bounce back and forth, not necessarily landing anywhere on the court of our current discussion.

As you can imagine, this didn't exactly endear me to my teachers. To be fair, I wasn't particularly impressed with them, either. My view of education was something along the lines of what I'd seen in *Dead Poet's Society*. I wanted instructors who would inspire me to think for myself, and to challenge existing views, not adults who expected us to read out of books and memorize facts. Most of my high school faculty, on the other hand, wondered why I couldn't remember and regurgitate details as well as my classmates. It seemed as if I was on the path to doom and failure… or at least a string of minimum wage jobs.

All of this might seem like it would be discouraging, or almost debilitating, but there was an upside. When I could find something that interested me, it was like a switch went on in my mind. I could achieve a state of hyperfocus that kept me engaged and engrossed for hours at a time. I would lock in and participate, learning more about a subject in an hour or two than my classmates would all year.

Over time, I figured out my goal wasn't to live as if I were on medication, but to harness the positive aspects of my mental machinery while also getting by in school. I needed to learn how to focus, even when doing so was difficult.

At this point, you might be wondering what any of this has to do with you. Unless you happen to have been born with ADHD yourself, or know someone close to you who is affected by it, this might all seem like a side plot on the way to building up *your* focus. However, there is probably a lot in my story that is more relevant to your life and career than you might realize. That's because our world is changing, and the way our minds deal with it is, too.

Our ADHD World

Even if you don't have ADHD, I bet you can relate to a lot of the symptoms I experience. Look at these statements and ask yourself how many of them apply to you occasionally, if not on a daily basis:

- I sometimes have trouble concentrating on the task or project that's right in front of me.
- I am often distracted by coworkers, my phone, or something on a computer screen.
- It's not unusual for me to work right up to a tight deadline, even if I'm worried about the consequences.
- I experience surges of motivation, followed by periods where I seem to get nothing done.

- I find it very difficult to focus on tasks that are repetitive or uninteresting.

No one but you knows how you are answering these questions, so it's okay to be honest. I am willing to bet, though, that 90% or more of the people reading this book are intimately familiar with these challenges (and don't worry, you can still benefit from what I'm going to show you even if these aren't persistent problems in your life or career).

Some of this comes down to human nature, of course, but a lot also has to do with the era you were lucky enough to be born in. A century ago it was obvious who had trouble with concentration. You could just look for the kid fidgeting at his desk. Now, *everyone* is that kid. In the age of cell phones, texts, social media alerts, and multitasking, more and more people are displaying ADHD symptoms… even if they don't have the brain chemistry to back it up.

You don't have to be as interested in focus as I am to notice how big of an issue this has become. Take a look around while you're driving. I bet you'll notice many (or even most) of your fellow motorists are fiddling with their phones. Some won't even be looking at the road all that often. The same applies to pedestrians. Faced with thousands of pounds of oncoming glass, steel, and horsepower, they'll risk their lives in stepping out into the street while playing animated games that offer no real-world reward.

As someone who regularly speaks and entertains in the college market, I've had a firsthand view of the mental carnage. It's hard enough for those of us who can remember life without smartphones to concentrate; for those in their teens and 20s, it can seem outright impossible.

I'll occasionally find myself fighting for audience attention when I'm in the midst of a hypnosis show on a college campus. Think about that for a moment: a school has paid thousands of dollars for me to come in and helped me out by providing state-of-the-art lights and audio. On top of that, the people watching me perform are witnessing what might be the most interesting possible human phenomenon (a full-blown hypnotic trance) being conducted on their classmates, who are being psychologically transformed into animals and orchestra conductors. And yet, I *still* have to make sure what I'm doing is engaging enough to keep them from their favorite social media app.

Don't take this to mean I'm bashing millennials. While that might be popular these days, my issue isn't with young people. In fact, I love the enthusiasm they bring to my shows and speeches. Instead, what I'm talking about is the most visible sign of a bigger epidemic. We live in an attention-deficit society. While students might be easiest to pick on, you've been in meetings and traffic jams that were made worse by distracted people. In fact, I can almost guarantee you've been on a flight where the pilot was checking his phone or had fallen asleep (go ahead and look it up, anonymous surveys back me up).

The point is *all of us* struggle with focus and concentration. It isn't just those of us with ADHD, and it isn't only when we are bored. People are going through their days in a constant state of distraction, even when their relationships, careers, and very lives are on the line.

In some ways, nature and technology are working against us. It's great that we live in an era where you can be connected at all times. We no longer worry about people being stranded by the side of the road, or experiencing a medical emergency, and having no way to contact others. All that communication comes at a cost, though. Every little text, email, or notification injects our minds with a tiny shot of dopamine. That means we look forward to the next one just a little more, and that it takes a lot more stimulus for us to actually feel engaged.

Also, the fact that we tweet, snap, and post on a continual basis encourages us to take on more than we can handle. It's easy to feel these days like you aren't living life to the fullest if you don't work out every morning, earn seven figures a year, and cook gourmet organic meals every night. Inspiration and friendly competition are wonderful things, but an overachieving lifestyle – one that leaves us feeling like we are being ripped into many directions at once – isn't healthy or productive.

We need new ways of living and being if we are going to cope. I might be the one with ADHD, but every time I look around I see the rest of the world catching up with me. I remember how amazed my friends were when they learned I could watch a movie three times in a row without moving a muscle. How could I be so entranced? The same question comes to me when I see dozens of people glued to their phones.

In fact, I sometimes wonder how things would turn

out for me if I were a child today. Would it be even harder to concentrate, with all the devices that are constantly beeping and vying for our attention? Or, would my natural tendency to do too many things at once just cause me to blend in?

I don't know the answer, but what I can say for sure is that there are millions and millions of people who could benefit from what I've learned through my own struggles with concentration. They may not have ADHD brain chemistry, but they are living in a world that nudges them towards never-ending distractions.

If you're one of them, or just want to get more done while feeling at-ease with your schedule, then you might need to think and act a little differently.

Why It's Time to Focus on Focus

Even though chaos is being forced upon us by the world at large, it doesn't mean we have to accept being distracted, tired, or stressed out. I would argue that the opposite is true – that we have a bigger opportunity to be aware of the challenges that are in front of us, and to live better lives as a result.

I meet a lot of people who take it as a foregone conclusion that they have to be distracted at all times. That's simply not the case. In fact, in our world, it's the small handful who can keep their eyes on the road, so to speak, who come out ahead. It's the ones who can stay zeroed in on their personal and professional goals who will reach their dreams. They simply refuse to be drawn away from the projects, or points of focus, that matter the most to them.

I truly believe this and think it's one of the keys to success in life. In his groundbreaking book, *Outliers*, the bestselling author Malcolm Gladwell observes that it takes around 10,000 hours to master any task or specialty. That's a lot of time, but not an insurmountable challenge. Going strictly by that math, you certainly *could* become one of the world's greatest at whatever it is you want to do. However, you'd have to be willing to give up a minimum of 40 hours per week for five years, or 20 hours per week for 10 years if it wasn't your full-time job.

What Gladwell was referring to is the mental equivalent of the phenomenon of accelerating returns. If you put enough money into a safe investment fund, the interest you make will eventually start earning more profits on its own, to the point that you'll become very wealthy over many years. If you devote enough time to a skill or specialty, you'll become familiar with it, then proficient, and eventually outstanding. That puts both the challenge and power of focus on display. You can accomplish almost anything if you concentrate your time and mental energy on it, but it's hard to get anything done if you are continually distracted.

Another benefit of focus is that it can draw you closer to what you love. The more you enjoy something, the easier it's going to be for you to give it your full attention. So, if you make a conscious decision to concentrate on goals and activities you really like, you'll get better and better at them while needing to do fewer things you don't enjoy.

For instance, I have spent many years of my life working on my speaking and entertainment skills. I can stand up at a moment's notice and give you a compelling hour-long presentation on focus, or deliver dozens of laughs with hypnosis and shock you with sleight-of-hand. It took me quite a bit of time and practice to develop those skills, of course, but now that I have them I can work on these things while paying other people to do my taxes or proofread my pages. Focus allows me to enjoy my working time more, and to have the freedom to pursue my passions.

Because the internet, global travel, and other modern phenomena have created so many possibilities, it's easy to mistake distractions for worthwhile goals. If you have a dozen different hobbies, like learning Mandarin on YouTube and taking salsa dancing classes once a month, you're probably having fun. And, you likely have a very interesting Instagram account. But if you're looking for long-term satisfaction and achievement, you might be better off focusing on one or two things instead of 10 or 20. That's how you make real headway and progress.

The world we live in requires us to be mentally flexible. We have to be able to change direction and adapt to new ideas or ways of thinking. However, that's not the same as saying we should be all over the place all the time. What you focus on will dictate the direction of your life, and the amount of success you find. Don't let anything distract you from that reality.

. . .

The Two Forms of Focus That Matter

Hopefully, I've impressed upon you that finding calm and concentration is an issue for everyone, not just those of us with a hunter's mind. And, I hope I've convinced you that searching for focus cannot only change your life, but permanently set you on a new and better course.

Assuming those two things are true, then the next step is to share with you my system for keeping a clear head and getting things done. The beauty of the approach I follow is that absolutely anyone can use it. After all, I'm a kind of worst-case scenario when it comes to concentration. I have the attention span of an infant, along with the memory of a gold fish, and I'm not afraid to admit it. If I can use the advice I'm going to give you to keep my mind on track, then I promise you can, too.

It hasn't been easy living in the modern world with the chemicals in my brain fighting my need for focus and concentration at every step. It has gotten easier over time, though. That's partly because I've gotten older, but also because I have learned what works for me when I need to keep my thoughts in line. There isn't any one single thing I do to manage my ADHD or motivation; instead, I follow a strategy with a handful of distinct parts. Each one is important to keeping me concentrating on whatever I need to be doing or thinking about at the moment.

Although the rest of this book is going to be devoted

to giving you my seven-step plan for maintaining concentration, I want to be careful to point out that it comes in two forms. And, if you're going to be successful in our ADHD world, you have to be able to manage both of them.

The first kind of focus is the one that's needed to stay engrossed in the task at hand. It's the mental power you might use to balance your checkbook, for example, when you'd rather be playing a game on your phone. Or, it might mean finishing a tough project when you want to be on social media. This is the classic aspect of mental clarity that people with attention deficit disorders can struggle with. However, almost anyone can struggle with concentration in today's world no matter how their brain is wired.

The second kind of focus is harder to observe directly, and even more crucial to your success in life. It has to do with the ability to keep yourself moving on a trajectory towards your biggest goals. This is the kind of focus or motivation that persuades you to have a fruit salad for breakfast instead of a giant stack of pancakes, or to put in that extra hour of work when you know your favorite television show is on.

This second type of focus tends to be a huge problem for men and women of all ages. That's because you don't need ADHD to realize that we all have too many competing dreams, ideas, and priorities in our lives. Some we give to ourselves, others are put upon us by family, employers, professors, or even society at large. In order to get where we really want to go, we have to develop the ability to decide what is important for ourselves and then stick to our guns.

These two types of focus are obviously related. If you can't concentrate on something that's right in front of you, you'll never make real progress towards your lifelong dreams. And, if you aren't consistent in the way you set your goals, then the activities you do day-to-day can't move you towards the life you really want. You need both sides of the equation to balance.

Are You Ready to Focus on What Matters to You?

As we move away from the problem of distraction and into my best advice for mental clarity, I hope you'll approach the ideas that are yet to come with an open mind. Understand some of the tools I'm going to share will seem simple or obvious at first, but most of the best advice in life follows that pattern. Even if you think you already know where I'm going, or why I recommend something, I encourage you to stick with it and read through each section at least once. That's right, I want you to start practicing focus by giving me your full concentration for the couple of hours it takes to finish this book.

After that, you might want to come back and re-read the whole thing, or sections that speak to you, as you turn these concepts into daily habits. Again, know that none of them are going to be complex, difficult, or expensive. They are just simple things that work because they fit well with the way your brain operates.

And finally, I want you to keep in mind that just as I'm not a character in a movie, neither are you. Even though you decide to make some changes in your life, you can't expect them to fully sink in and show results right away. There are going to be setbacks, moments of confusion, and times when old routines set in. That's fine. It can be difficult to re-train your brain to concentrate, but the benefits are worth it.

Your mind is like a muscle. Right now, it might be out of shape from all the digital fast food you've been giving it. But with a steady diet of good ideas, positive reinforcement, and a tiny bit of mental exercise, you can get your brain back into shape. Then you'll find concentration comes to you more easily, and you can focus (with great results) for longer periods of time. That's when you really start to fly and begin to see all kinds of wonderful improvements in your life.

Let's take the next step together. Turn the page and see what you can do to improve your powers of focus right now.

THREE

Do More of What You Love

I sat silently and smiled to myself while a grown man hurled expletives in my face. It was one of the happiest moments of my life.

The setting was a family restaurant, and I'd just performed one of my first magic tricks as a "professional," haven been given a few extra dollars by one of the establishment's managers to entertain parents and children as part of a promotion.

I should probably explain at this point that hearing a dirty word is often the ultimate compliment for a magician. Anytime some version of: "You [BAD WORD]! How in the [WORSE WORD] did you do that?" graces your ears, things are going well.

On this particular occasion, I was especially pleased because I had only been practicing magic for a few months. But, I had been practicing a *lot.* Between classes and shifts at my other jobs – I had nearly two dozen of them during my college career because I would move on after getting bored with whatever I was doing at the time

– I would be practicing with cards, coins, and even silverware. I worked at my illusions endlessly, refining the finer points and drilling myself again and again until I could perform each one blindfolded if I had to.

At the time, I wasn't attempting to build towards any kind of paid appearance or specific opportunity. I was just following a newfound passion. Eventually, someone saw me do a trick and asked if I could perform a few more while people had dinner. I thought I could, and that led to the blue language I can't specifically describe in this book.

Because that first paying gig led to others, and then dozens and hundreds of more, it turned out being a big breakthrough in my career. However, it also taught me a very important lesson about focus: it's a lot easier to pay attention when you're concentrating on something you're interested in.

Don't Fight Your Nature

I've already mentioned that there were a lot of things about school I hated. I didn't enjoy reading, or memorizing facts and figures. Some of that was required to get my degree, but a lot of it felt useless and empty at the time. If I'm being honest, it still does.

Topics like magic and hypnotism, on the other hand, could keep me occupied for several hours at a time. They ignited my curiosity and brought me into a state of hyperfocus. Even to this day, I can lose huge periods of time learning a new trick or mastering a routine for a stage show. There are just so many fun and interesting things that happen along the way that it's almost impossible to get bored.

I'm sure you also have activities in your life that you really enjoy. They might be very different from the things that excite me, but that part isn't important. What matters is that your focus will improve if you find a way to do more of what you love.

It's so much easier to concentrate when you enjoy whatever it is you're concentrating on. This is one of the basic foundations of focus and productivity, but it's easy to lose sight of in today's world. That's because so many of us are expected to be everything. We feel like we have to be great at cooking, housecleaning, managing money, and half a dozen other professional tasks. In reality, our nature usually steers us towards some activities over others. We can't necessarily avoid *all* of what makes us feel bored, but why wouldn't you devote the majority of your time and effort to the things that make you feel engrossed?

Somewhere out there, I can imagine there is an accountant reading this book who simply loves numbers. Or, maybe there's a history professor who can't get enough of names, dates, and details. Their passions are very different from mine, and they don't necessarily struggle with ADHD. What each of us has in common, though, is that we'll be happier and more productive doing things that are a good match for our interests.

I often find that I'm most distractible when I'm slaving away at something like laundry or housecleaning. I don't enjoy these tasks, so it's easy for my mind to wander. That's true of all of us. If you could devote most of your time to things you find truly fascinating, you would find that a lot of problems related to focus and goal setting would disappear.

Passion is Energizing and Engaging

Have you ever found yourself staying up until the middle of the night to keep at something even though you know you should go to bed?

We all have. Usually when this occurs it's for one of two reasons – either we are facing a stiff and immovable deadline (like the one to file our taxes), or we feel so entranced with a game or project that we just can't pull ourselves away. This, in essence, is how self-hypnotism works, and it can be powerful. When truly engaged in an activity, your brain can literally lose track of time. A few hours can go by like a couple of minutes, and you can be making great progress the whole time.

Why is it that we don't run out of energy or focus during these periods of intense activity? How can it be that your eyes feel bleary when you're staring at receipts at 11 PM on April 15, but not when you find yourself at a high-stakes poker table at four in the morning?

The answer is that active focus, the rush you get from concentrating on something you're actually enjoying, is incredibly energizing. You might eventually wear down when you're in this state, but it's more likely that you'll simply run out of time (or into responsibilities). In other words, the consequences of ignoring the rest of the world will get to be too great, so you'll reluctantly turn your attention elsewhere. That's when the fatigue sets in.

This type of engagement is addictive. That's not necessarily a great thing if you're gambling or playing video games, but it's a wonderful force for productivity when you find an activity that really suits you. Each new hyperfocused session makes you more and more excited, leading you to try harder and dig deeper. Your progress builds on itself and you feel like you can't wait to get to work on the project that's holding your attention with an iron grip.

Another interesting byproduct of being focused on what you're doing is that you give off an energy that's attractive to other people. I don't necessarily mean that in a romantic sense, although it certainly can apply.

When you're having a great time, others can tell and want to participate… or at least be around you because you're so committed to whatever is in front of you. This is why great leaders are almost always personally invested in the groups and causes they support. The people around them can detect their enthusiasm on a subconscious level and begin to feed into it.

This great mixture of energy and magnetism can't come into play until you find something that really drives you, though. It's almost impossible, from a psychological standpoint, to get that deeply engaged into something you find boring or irrelevant. In fact, the opposite tends to happen very quickly.

Willpower is Limited

Willpower is one of those words that gets used a lot, and usually incorrectly. That's because people talk about having a ton of willpower as if it's a wonderful thing. It can be, for short periods of time, but you might not actually want too much of it.

To understand why, we have to look at what it really represents. Motivation is the force that pushes you to chase what you love and achieve what matters in your life. Willpower, on the other hand, is a strength to endure tasks and experiences you would rather avoid. That's why, for example, it takes a lot of willpower to stay on a diet. You don't love the idea of eating salad constantly, you simply avoid things you like more to get a certain long-term result. You're probably already aware that this doesn't work very often.

It's not hard to figure out the reason. Some of us have more willpower than others, but we all work with limited quantities. The more of it we use, the less we have to throw around. You can recharge your willpower somewhat by getting a good night's sleep or having a relaxing vacation, but doing things you really don't enjoy isn't a long-term way to stay happy, healthy, or productive.

When willpower runs out our subconscious minds take over. The emotional parts of our brains start looking for things that feel more comfortable. The subconscious may even overcompensate in an effort to balance things out. For example, it's amazing how often a two-day juice fast turns into a late-night chocolate cake binge.

The answer to this problem isn't to get an endless

supply of willpower. That isn't possible for most people, and even if it was, it could have dire long-term results. Too much self-control can lead to situations where you don't follow your instincts or passions. Over the course of months and decades, that can leave you with a lot of regrets.

The better solution is to simply make an effort to rearrange your life in a way that's more consistent with your interests and values. In other words, do more of what you love and causes you joy than the things that you don't enjoy and lead to stress. One tends to make you happier, healthier, and more successful; the other leaves you tired and unfocused.

If you need to lose weight and get in shape, find healthier foods you enjoy and exercise you can look forward to. To move your career forward in the right direction, don't try to burn your precious and limited focus on jobs or projects that don't energize you. Point your talents in a direction that will yield better mental, emotional, intangible results.

Willpower is limited, but to me that's a good thing. It stops us from moving in the wrong direction too often and reminds us to chase more of our passions.

Turn Chores into Fun Games and Projects

Sadly, despite all of my wise words and sage advice, I can't help you avoid every unpleasant task or chore in your life. If you're like most of us, you're going to find yourself in a situation where you have to pick up the dry cleaning, clean out the gutters, or do something else you really can't stand. But, that doesn't mean you have to let boredom or disinterest sap your focus. You can decide to make the job into a game instead.

Many years ago, during my stint where I was trying every form of employment I could think of, I found myself working at a pizza shop. It wasn't a bad job. I liked my coworkers, and there was plenty of great food to eat.

One aspect of the work really annoyed me, though. At the end of the night, after all the pies at been served and delivered, I was responsible for folding pizza boxes for the next day. It was the kind of repetitive busywork that drives someone with ADHD crazy. On a busy Saturday night, we could go through hundreds of take-out and delivery orders. That meant a huge chunk of time working on something I couldn't stand. To make it worse, there usually wasn't time to finish until I was almost ready to go home. That meant folding boxes when I was already tired after a long night while all of my friends were out on dates or at parties.

I hated folding those pizza boxes with a passion until I discovered a secret – one that has served me well in the many years since. Rather than dreading the chore, I turned it into a challenge. Instead of focusing on folding the boxes one by one, I started seeing how many I could do in a minute. Then, I tried to figure out whether I could knock them out by a certain time, rewarding myself with a small treat if I were able to meet the deadline.

These were just silly mental games, of course, but they turned an activity I despised into something that I could often enjoy. It got to the point that my coworkers, seeing how quickly I would fold the boxes, remarked on how much I must have enjoyed my side work. The truth was quite the opposite, of course, but the fact that they couldn't tell the difference showed how well it was working. I got the added benefit of getting praise and recognition from my boss for being a proactive employee… all because I figured out how to make a game from something I hated.

In life, there are going to be some things you have to do even though you don't want to. If you can turn these activities into a game, you may find that they annoy you a lot less. At the very least, you'll get through them faster and will probably do a better job than you would have otherwise.

What happens, though, when you truly cannot manage to enjoy something that is a necessary part of your day or career? I have a last resort answer for that, too.

Motivate Yourself by What You Hate

Once I got good enough to perform magic and hypnotism for money, there was a wonderful and unexpected side effect. Namely, that I didn't have to keep other jobs when I was getting paid to do what I loved.

Before long, I had quit my normal jobs to take on more performances. Then, the money got to be good enough (and steady enough) that I was able to hire professionals to help with things like marketing and bookkeeping. With each passing year, I've been able to devote more and more time to the parts of my career I like, and fewer hours to tasks that I find repetitive or uninteresting.

Over time, I've been able to duplicate this process again and again. The most successful people I know have taken it to further extremes. Meet enough millionaires, and you'll find that the majority of them won't mow their own lawns or fix their own sinks. A lot of them don't even do their own shopping. They put themselves into situations where their time is worth too much to handle these chores on their own. But also, avoiding these tasks is a big driving force that helps them keep moving forward.

In other words, you can use things you hate as powerful motivators.

Let me give you an example. I can't stand doing laundry. Everything about it bores me. But, it needs to be done and I'm not at a point in my career (yet) where I feel like I can justify paying somebody else to do it for me. So, whenever I'm faced with a full hamper, I go ahead and do it. As I do, though, I tell myself the entire time that soon I'll be successful enough to outsource this particular job, not to mention a few others. Just the thought of it pushes me to work a little bit harder.

You might not hate laundry, but I bet you have some chores or professional duties you'd like to get rid of. Accomplish enough of what you love and care about and you can reach the point where you can turn them into someone else's problem. Then, you'll have one less distraction and another reason to improve your focus.

. . .

Fun is Focusing and Productive

As the old saying goes, if you find a job you love you'll never work a day in your life. I don't know that any of us ever really gets to a point where we have nothing but enjoyable tasks to focus on, but I do know that too many people devote their precious time and energy to things that make them feel tired instead of energized.

Why not enjoy yourself more instead? It's easier, it's more fun, and it's certainly more likely to drive you to accomplishing your personal and professional goals. Life's too short to waste time on anything that feels like a waste. Why not do more of what you love?

FOUR

Control Your Environment

Working as a hypnotist and speaker, I'm used to being up late at night. It's not unusual for me to wrap up a show past midnight and then pack up to drive to an airport or hotel.

All that late-night travel used to worry my father. He was constantly telling me to be careful about the road, other drivers, and all the hidden dangers I couldn't see. That's good advice, of course, but the truth is I *love* driving at night. It's dark and all I can see is what's in front of my headlights. There isn't anything to focus on except for what's right in front of you. It's hard to be distracted by signs and scenery when they aren't in your field of vision.

The things that might otherwise distract me when I'm driving during the late and early hours are still there, of course, but they sit just outside the reach of my headlights. To my mind, they might as well not be there at all. That's the kind of tunnel vision we should all be striving for in our day-to-day lives. We want to focus on the things that are important to us, or that are urgent and require our immediate attention. Everything else can and should be put to the side.

Most of us don't live our lives as if we're driving at night. We take our eyes off the road constantly, being pulled from one thought or idea to another, even if it slows the progress we could be making towards our bigger goals. In this chapter, I'm going to share my best advice for controlling your environment and, by extension, your focus. The fewer distractions you have in front of you, the easier it becomes to find calm and concentration.

Let's start with the most obvious step you can take right away…

Remove Distractions from Your Eyesight

Sometimes, the biggest step you can take towards getting things done is controlling your physical environment (or at least what's right in front of you). For instance, if I need to write something for my business, or focus on a contract, I might begin by cleaning off my desk.

This might seem like procrastination, and it can be if you're using household chores as busywork. However, I have often found that it's much easier to focus on what's in front of me if it's the *only* thing in front of me.

In other words, keeping your desk clean helps you to concentrate on one item at a time. Likewise, picking up your bedroom, or tidying up your car, can let you feel more relaxed and creative. Psychological researchers have backed this up with studies and surveys. When you have things that are out of place in your surroundings, it takes a little bit of mental energy to be aware of them. Your productivity increases when items that could otherwise be clamoring for your attention are tucked away in their proper places.

None of this is to say you have to be obsessively clean. If you were to stop by my home and see my desk, for example, you would find that it's often in disarray when I'm not working on a specific project. And, while my home office might be clean, that's not to say my bedroom necessarily will be. I control my environment so I can be productive when I have to work, but I don't go overboard because that's not the way my personality works. I'm not bothered by a little bit of clutter as long as it's not in the way of what I'm trying to do.

Creating the right environment for focus isn't just about tidying up your home or work space. It also involves choosing where to be when you have things that have to be taken care of. When I was younger, I would make a point of sitting in the front of a classroom. It was easier for me to lock in on a professor if I couldn't see other students around me. You might find the same approach works for you in a study hall or meeting room. Position yourself in a place where you'll have the fewest distractions.

In the same way, I sometimes find it easier to work in a coffee shop than I do my house. There are still distractions, but they aren't personal. At home I might notice something that's upcoming on my calendar or get a visit from a friend. But for all the clanking and chatter that happens in a public space, it's easy to ignore because none of it is directed specifically to me. For instance, right now I'm on an airplane writing this book and am completely locked into my words and thoughts.

You might have to experiment with this concept a little bit to find out what works for you, but the better you can get at removing distractions from your line of sight, the easier it will be for you to focus on one thing at a time.

Minimize Interruptions and Temptations

It only makes sense that you have to minimize distractions and interruptions if focus is your goal, but that's not the way most of the people I see live their lives. In fact, I would say a lot of them act as if they want to be pulled away from their goals at any given time.

For example, I recently picked up a friend of mine so we could have lunch together. When I walked into the office where he works as a financial advisor, I couldn't help but notice they had a television on in the background. It was tuned to a cable show where the hosts talked about stocks and bonds. It's good that they had on something that was relevant to their industry, I guess, but you can't convince me having a nonstop parade of talking heads pulling at your attention is the best way to concentrate on managing someone's money.

When you place distractions in your own environment, you're essentially saying that whatever you have interrupting you is more important than the thing you're doing or working towards. That's almost never the case. Instead, keeping the distractions around lets us get away with ignoring something that might be difficult or require tough decisions. We convince ourselves that we are "busy" because there's lots going on, when in reality we aren't really doing anything.

In that way, many of our distractions are really just temptations. Have you ever had a friend who decided to lose weight but kept lots of chips, sweets, and other snacks in their cupboards? I know I've gone through this myself. When I was *really* serious about getting fit I threw all of that stuff out. It hurt a bit because I had spent money on those items and I was looking forward to eating them. I finally realized, though, that seeing them constantly was holding me back.

With unhealthy treats in the house there would be a constant voice in my head telling me: look at the chocolate just staring at you. You've been good. You deserve it. How bad would it be to just eat one bar?

That would go on until finally I would just eat it. It was easy to give in because it was convenient.

Sometimes, we can even use other people as convenient distractions from what we are doing. It's difficult, but I've had to get into the habit of sometimes telling friends and colleagues that I'll have to call them back when they reach out to me. It isn't that those relationships aren't important, but that non-emergency calls need to take a backseat to other priorities. Get in the habit of doing that and your own friends and family members will start to realize how important focus is to you and will train themselves to only interrupt you when it's important or they know you aren't in the middle of something. You're also training yourself to focus, which is just as important.

This is a good place to add a reminder that some interruptions are inevitable. In my business, for instance, a call from my agent will almost always take precedence over whatever else I am doing. Dates can be booked quickly, and if I'm not available some other speaker or entertainer could get the work. You may have parts of your job or life that are like that. It's perfectly understandable if you have to deal with those interruptions – none of us is completely focused all the time.

Move forward with the mindset that you're going to minimize interruptions, distractions, and temptations. Then, you aren't going to let yourself be pulled away from an important task or project very often. You'll set up your environment so your attention stays on what's in front of you.

Ideally, that would be the last word on the matter. However, there is a special kind of distraction I want to address directly.

Using Technology to Enhance Your Concentration

There are a lot of really wonderful things about the technology we have today. Things that were only seen in the science fiction movies I watched in my father's store as a kid are all around us now. With a couple presses of a button I can speak to friends and family around the globe, get an answer to a question that's on my mind, or just be entertained by the endless creativity of others. Or, I can throw cartoon birds at pigs. That's fun, too.

But really, that's the point. All this convenience comes at a cost. At a time when I should be working on an important goal or priority, I am literally milliseconds away from speaking to any of my friends or family, researching the answer to a question that has floated into my mind, or being entertained by the endless creativity of others. Hopefully you get the point, and the irony. Technology can help us to achieve great things, but it can also serve as an enormous distraction that stops us from focusing on what actually matters.

So, how do we train ourselves to use technology in a productive way that aids our concentration instead of killing it? As with most things, it starts with having the right intention.

It doesn't take a lot of effort to clear your desk, or part of it, so you can devote your attention to a task that's right in front of you. It requires even less willpower and energy to change the settings on your phone so you aren't receiving constant notifications about incoming text messages and social media updates. It's hard to get anything done if you have a device sitting just inches away that pings or vibrates every time someone wants you to shift your mind to something that matters to them. Hard as it might be to believe, I promise the world won't end if you ignore your updates and notifications for a while.

You could take this a step further, as some people I know do, and keep entirely separate devices for work and personal use. That way, one can be setup without your personal accounts, and can be kept almost entirely silent. Or, you could simply change your settings on a single device so that you are only interrupted if there is an emergency... like a new tweet from Eric Mina (I'm mostly just kidding).

There are even certain apps you can use that will help you focus by building lists, managing deadlines, and setting priorities in your daily calendar. I'm going to tackle these in the next chapter, but I just want you to remember that technology doesn't have to be distracting; it only seems that way because that's how most of us use it.

It's not always easy to change your phone habits. Psychologists agree, with overwhelming evidence, that our devices are addictive. They are like digital crack. We get small little bursts in the pleasure centers of our brain when receiving texts, tweets, and messages. But far too often these interruptions are the mental equivalent of fast food, alcohol, or drugs – they feel good in the moment but rob us of our capacity for concentration and goal achievement over time.

Ask yourself a question: when was the last time you got a notification on your phone that was more important than the dreams you have for your life? How often does letting a screen interrupt you actually make you happier? If we're being honest we all know the answers, and that changing the way we use our phones and computers could help us stay more focused and positive.

Clearing Your Space and Your Mind

Why is it we always tend to have too much going on at any given moment? I think we can find the answer by looking at the world we live in, as well as our own habits and priorities. Far too often we aren't actually serious about accomplishing the things we say we dream of. If we were, we wouldn't allow ourselves to be distracted by so many little things that get in the way.

Martin Luther King Jr. once said: "Take the first step in faith. You don't have to see the whole staircase, just take the first step." He was referring to the dreams of those protesting for and participating in the civil rights movement, of course, but that quote has always struck me as being a beautiful illustration of the power of focus. When you know what you have to accomplish in the moment to reach a higher goal, you can let the rest of the world fade away.

In a study done in the UK, a group of psychology students and researchers found that a person who was high on marijuana could generally function more effectively than another person who was multitasking. Before you tell your boss or professor I'm giving you permission to blaze up, understand the point isn't about the drug; it's that your mind is even less sharp than you realize when you're dealing with distractions and interruptions. You simply aren't at your best, and you aren't getting things done.

We can prove this pretty easily. Stop and think about two things at once. They can be any two things you want, like the Statue of Liberty and the quadratic equation. Or, think of the main street in your hometown and the way I'd look in a Speedo (don't pretend you weren't thinking it (wait... no one wants to think about that. But it's in your mind now. Isn't hypnosis fun?).

If you attempted this for more than a couple of seconds you learned two valuable facts. First, that I look great in swimwear. Second, that your mind can't simultaneously focus on more than one thing at a time. It simply flickers back and forth between them, getting more and more fatigued along the way. Imagine what happens when you try to concentrate on three things, or five, or more than that.

Multitasking slows you down and keeps you from giving an important task or thought the attention it needs. You think you're doing many things faster, but in reality you're just making everything worse and more time-consuming.

This, to me, is an under-appreciated aspect of focus. Distractions slow you down. If you happen to be doing something unpleasant, why not get it done quickly so you can move on to something else you enjoy more? And why not concentrate and finish it correctly so you don't have to repeat the task again or suffer the consequences of doing a bad job?

If dealing with interruptions is more harmful than most people realize, focusing on one task at a time has greater benefits, too. Just as small diversions can be addictive, so can the process of entering a flow state where you are relaxed, creative, and productive. Once your mind reaches that zone, things seem to happen all on their own. You get better and sharper, even though you seem to be putting in less effort. That's a beautiful way to work and live, but it only happens when you're locked in on a specific project or process.

Focusing your attention doesn't mean tuning out the rest of the world forever. You can still make plenty of time for your friends, your favorite shows or hobbies, and even your phone. It's all about being time-oriented so you can put your mind in the right gear to stay on task and bring out the best version of yourself.

It might not be easy to control your environment and clear away distractions if you aren't used to it, but the payoff is enormous. You'll be more productive at work or at school. At the same time, you'll enjoy your downtime more, as well, because you won't be thinking about all the other things you should be working on while you're having fun.

FIVE

Staying Focused With Lists and Priorities

Have you ever had the experience of going to the store and forgetting what you left the house to get? Having ADHD is like that, except it can happen anywhere and anytime. I can forget what I wanted from the refrigerator when I open it, why I called someone as the phone rings, or even where I was driving when I get off an exit. It's a minor miracle I didn't forget what this book was about halfway through.

There is an old saying that goes something like this: the faintest ink is better than the strongest memory. I couldn't agree more. We live in a time when it's easier than ever to record your thoughts at a moment's notice. We also live in a world where we're surrounded by distractions on an almost constant basis. Keeping track of your most important tasks, priorities, and deadlines is a great way to keep yourself moving in the right direction.

As it turns out, lists and priorities aren't just for organization. They can also help you to clear your mind and focus on whatever happens to be important to you at the time. In this chapter, I'm going to share my most important reasons why. As always, I'll be blending a bit of common sense with ideas I've picked up studying psychology and performance over the years, along with a few personal observations… if I can remember them. I'm not sure I wrote them down. I wish I could have had this book to help me write this book, but I feel like that would have created some sort of sci-fi paradox that would end the world.

Rather than dwelling on my time travel conundrum, let's get started with the importance of written notes themselves.

My List of Lists

I use a lot of different lists to keep my life organized and my mind focused. Some of them are for little things that would be easy to overlook, while others help me to bridge the gaps between my long-term goals and immediate priorities.

To give you a sense of how this looks in the real world, here are some of the lists I rely on regularly…

- My speaking and performing schedule
- A list of work activities I need to finish for the day
- Another list of personal things I want to get done in my free time
- My list of ongoing projects that need to be started or finished

- A shopping list for groceries, online purchases, etc.
- My enemies and how I'll get revenge on them (sadly I'm a pacifist and humanist, so this one goes very much unfinished)

You probably have lists like these, too, even if you haven't kept them written down (especially the enemies list). They represent the sort of notes and reminders we all need to keep little things from slipping our minds.

The most important list I keep isn't one that fits this profile, though. It's a set of ideas I use for *dream building*, and I try to look at it at least once a day. In this document I have a set of longer-range plans that are big priorities for me. It's the list that helps me fill in the other lists.

On my dream list are goals like making a million dollars per year, earning a black belt in Brazilian jiu-jitsu and judo, buying my dream home, speaking for 10,000 people or more, and visiting every continent. It amounts to what some people might call a vision board, and its role is to help me stay inspired, to keep moving towards the kinds of accomplishments that make me feel excited for the future. It's like a bucket list, but without the impending sense of death hanging over it.

Naturally, items from my dream list become projects that need to be finished. Then, these work their way into my daily "to do" lists for my business and personal life. Some might even translate into things that have to be bought and end up on my shopping list. The point is that I never put together a list of things to do without having a bigger meaning or goal attached to them. I want to move my life forward, not create busywork for myself.

Likewise, I try not to go to the store simply to buy food or something else I want. Instead, I shop with my fitness and focus goals in mind so I can keep temptations and distractions out of my life.

Putting together all of these lists was a chore at first. I got tired of typing and writing everything down. Before long, though, it became a system. My mind started doing this automatically and as a result I knew where to look for the information I needed and stopped forgetting important details.

That's exactly the way you want to work, too. I'm going to show you why in just a minute. First, though, we need to talk about how you're going to keep all of these different lists together and in a usable format.

How to Keep Your Lists

Obviously, there isn't any single "right" way to keep track of things like shopping lists and vision boards. You could write them down on a piece of paper, keep a special notebook, or type away in a long word processing document.

However, I prefer to let technology do the hard work. So, I tend to rely on apps that are on my phone or tablet. That makes the process fast and easy so it only takes a few seconds to record a thought. And, because I almost always have my phone with me, there is little chance I'll forget about my thought before I write it down. There are exceptions, however. In some cases, I may even keep a notebook with me and then record those thoughts digitally when it's convenient.

There are a couple of big benefits to this approach. One is that it makes your ideas easier to organize, combine, and review. The other is that cloud technology makes it possible for you to backup all of your lists and keep them in a digitally safe and secure place. If ink is better than memory, then a secure, encrypted, and backed up server is preferable to a notebook that can get lost, be left in an airport, or be destroyed by a little bit of rain or snow.

The only downside is potentially turning over my information to SkyNet. If the terminators ever come to get us, they'll know right where to find me at any given day or time. Still, I feel like a convenient digital system makes the convenience worth more than that very significant risk.

That being said, the best system for organizing your lists is the one you'll use every day. And, you can always make a switch later. Like all the advice I have to give you, what matters is that you put a plan into action immediately. If you're comfortable writing things down in a small notebook you can carry in your pocket, then begin by doing that. Start making a list of things to buy or do right now. You can spend an hour or two improving your list system later. That's not nearly as critical as putting the concept to use and beginning immediately.

Remember that focus and achievement are all about habits. Once you get accustomed to jotting down a thought immediately as it comes to you, your life will get easier and you'll start to be more productive. That's not just my opinion, it's a solid fact. The reason has to do with the way our minds handle information, attention, and loose mental threads.

The Upshot of Using Detailed Lists and Schedules

Just making a few lists probably won't change your life in a significant way. If you can get into the habit of doing so, however, and develop a system that becomes secondhand, there are enormous benefits.

The most immediate one goes back to the tendency I mentioned in the opening to this chapter. I might forget what I'm supposed to be doing at a given moment more often than most people who don't have ADHD, but I know it's a problem for almost everyone I know. It's easy to get distracted and lose track of what you were working on or concentrating on in a moment. When you have a daily list or schedule in front of you, it's much easier to get back on track after an interruption.

Also, making lists and jotting down notes about your goals forces you to prioritize. That's important because none of us has enough time and energy to do all of the things we would like. There simply isn't enough of us, or sufficient hours in the day, to go around and cloning seems unlikely to solve the problem in the near future. So, we have to decide what we're going to actually do in the here and now and which ideas will be put off until later. It's better to make hard choices than it is to feel as if you aren't making progress on any of your dreams.

In some cases, this kind of thinking can prevent roadblocks and bottlenecks from holding us back. For instance, I had some remodeling done on my house a while ago. In the middle this process, a plumber couldn't make it out to my home for a few days. Suddenly, I found out the other people I'd hired to work on the job (electricians, drywall guys, etc.) were all stuck. They couldn't continue their work until he had finished his portion. It just wouldn't have made sense to seal up a wall, or install wiring, until we were sure running water wouldn't come gushing out unexpectedly.

A lot of things in life are like that. Projects have to follow a certain order or they take a lot longer or can't be finished at all. As the old saying goes, nine women can't make a baby in a month. By making lists and putting your thoughts in order, you can figure out how one step logically has to follow another.

Even if a specific order or timeline isn't important to your biggest goals, having lots of written notes that you check frequently might stop you from missing important dates or details. Before I put an organizational system into place – and actually started using it – I found myself paying late fees on memberships, utility bills, and other expenses. Being on the road for dozens of days every month, it was easy for me to forget about those sorts of things until I would have a few days off.

The problem is that those details add up. Not only can you cost yourself hundreds or thousands of dollars per year by failing to pay attention to due dates, but you can unintentionally miss out on birthdays, celebrations, concerts, and other fun activities. People tend to think of getting organized as a boring and tedious activity, but it's a great way to get more of what you actually want in your life.

However, the biggest benefit of integrating a list and organization system into your life is one people tend to overlook completely.

Using Lists for Focus

It's entirely possible that you've never realized the biggest benefit to keeping lists. Most people think they are about simple reminders, but remembering to make an important phone call or pick up butter from the grocery store is just beginning. Once you make your organizational system a real part of your life something amazing happens: you start to feel free in a way you didn't before.

Whether you realize it or not, all the extra thoughts you hold onto while trying to remember different details in your life are like mental furniture crammed into a small space. They make it hard for your mind to move around and express itself. There is always a sense, in the back of your brain, that you might be forgetting about something important. It's the psychological equivalent of having a splinter.

How powerful can these distractions be? Often, sleep specialists will recommend a patient with severe insomnia keep a notebook beside their bed. That way, they can record the thoughts they feel buzzing around inside of them. Once those ideas have been saved – and the person feels safe knowing they can come back to them later – anxiety and sleeplessness will often disappear. In other words, unresolved loops in your brain can keep you awake. One of the most beneficial ideas I give my clients is to write in a journal every night. Once you get all these thoughts out of your head you can sleep peacefully.

An even bigger problem with unaddressed thoughts is that they can also stop you from focusing entirely on what's in front of you. Imagine for a moment you have an important task that's pressing and needs to be finished immediately. However, you *also* know that later you need to remember an important appointment or family responsibility. Some small percentage of your mental horsepower is going to be devoted to remembering the obligation even though it isn't currently a concern. You can make it disappear from your mind by programming an alert into your phone or simply making a note you can be sure you'll see later.

When I first started touring as a hypnotist and speaker, my father was interested in my travel schedule. He loved that I was going to interesting places like California or Florida, and always wanted to know the details of my itinerary. Most of the time, I could recall which bookings were on my schedule, but not the cities where my connecting flights took me. "How could you not know this?" he would ask. The answer was simple – I was tuning out the details intentionally. Until I left for the airport, the information about specific layovers wasn't important. It would have just been mental clutter that kept me from focusing on more urgent or important priorities.

This might seem like a small point until you realize people without good organizational skills can have literally hundreds of random thoughts and "someday" aspirations occupying their thoughts. Then, they wonder why they have trouble concentrating or are completely stressed out.

When you get organized with lists, you clear all of this confusion out of your head. You relieve your brain of the stress it takes to try to remember dozens of little things that aren't pertinent at the moment but might be someday. That allows you to be more unencumbered and creative. You can focus on finding new solutions and connections when you need them instead of worrying about whether you'll forget about your dry-cleaning or the electric bill.

If you want to clear your mind, take away the obstacles that cloud your thinking. Start making lists and notes, and then come back to them on a daily or weekly basis. Over time, your brain will trust you to review the thoughts it has stored and your thoughts will start to feel lighter and clearer.

Turning Lists into Possibilities

In the early 1900s, Charles Schwab was the richest man in the world. Obsessed with the concept of productivity, he consulted with an expert named Ivy Lee to figure out how he could get more done in his busy days. Lee told his wealthy client that he could distill the most important piece of time management advice into one simple tip. I'm going to summarize it here:

Make a list of the most important things you have to do each day, beginning with the item that is most critical. Then, when you start working in the morning, concentrate on that task and ignore everything else until it's finished.

For that 15 minutes of advice, Schwab paid the advisor the equivalent of nearly half a million dollars and was said to have felt it was a wonderful value. He realized just how much power there was in the notion of focusing your energy on a single thing that could actually change your life.

I couldn't agree with this sentiment more. Without real targets and priorities, it's difficult to keep track of which direction we are headed, much less what we have to do to live our dreams.

It's a strange truth of life that most people will slightly overestimate what they can get done in a single day, but greatly underestimate what is possible for them in a year. You may have experienced this yourself. You begin the morning with all kinds of big plans and dreams, only to discover that small distractions and unexpected disruptions throw you off track. By the time evening comes, you've only accomplished two or three of the things you set out to finish.

Look farther down the road, though, and you'll see that you can do really amazing things if you commit to making a small but continuous effort. In just 12 months or less, people have lost more than 100 pounds. They've learned new languages. Many have started brand-new companies and careers or gone from being couch potatoes to endurance athletes.

Take that thinking a little farther and you'll discover you have the ability within you to do the kinds of things most people only daydream about. You could get the home you've always wanted to live in, travel around the world, become an expert in your field, or write a series of books.

All of this is possible, but it requires you to think bigger and find a way to maintain your focus from one hour and day to the next. Making lists and priorities a part of your regular routine is an important step in that direction.

SIX

Create a Sense of Urgency

I can still vividly remember what it was like to step into Times Square on a brisk Friday afternoon. It was early in my entertainment career. I was bright-eyed and ready to show off my hypnotism skills to the world. Armed with an irrational sense of optimism and a few routines I could practice on tourists, I was ready to light New York on fire with my mesmerizing mix of mind power and comedic instincts.

My debut ended before it could even begin.

I was looking for a shortcut to Broadway (and by extension, my destiny to become the world's best-known hypnotic entertainer. What I found instead was a man walking around with a sign on his back advertising a hypnosis show nearby. In less than a minute I realized someone else had already taken up the space I wanted to fill.

It was devastating for the first few moments. Then I remembered that all the great movie heroes endure setbacks. Besides, if one hypnotist could fill a show in the Big Apple, why couldn't two? A quick conversation with the sandwich board man revealed he wasn't the hypnotist who was performing. Still, he was willing to point me in the direction of the club that had hired him. So, I regathered my determination and marched over to the establishment so I could introduce myself.

Luckily, the club owner was inside and willing to meet with me. But, it only took a few moments for me to run into my next roadblock – he wasn't interested in booking another hypnotism act. He already had one he liked. However, if I were interested in doing a magic show he might be willing to give me a shot. Having a Times Square booking was better than not having a Times Square booking, so I started asking questions. It turned out the owner would audition me if I could get some people to show up and buy a couple of drinks. His next free afternoon was in two weeks.

I thanked the comedy club owner profusely and shook his hand. Then, when I walked outside, I had what I imagined to be a minor stroke. That's because I knew something he didn't: *I didn't have a magic show.*

Nothing Motivates Like a Deadline

At this point I should rewind the movie a bit and come clean. By this early point in my career I had gotten paid to perform magic in restaurants. I had even managed to score a few birthday parties. But I knew the simple tricks I used to entertain kids for their parents wasn't going to cut it in Times Square. I also knew the kind of opportunity I had in front of me didn't come around every day.

With two weeks in front of me and my dream of performing in New York City on the line, I had a couple of choices: I could either move into action or accept defeat and hope the chance would come around again someday. I didn't want to waste the opportunity, so I bet I could learn some new skills, improve my routine, *and* find a handful of people who would watch me perform in a hurry.

Some people would undoubtedly think that was a foolish decision, and it's true I could've ended up in a spot where I might have failed or been embarrassed. But so what? In my mind, that would have been far better than knowing I had a chance to audition for a club owner in Times Square and had let it pass me by because I was afraid of what might happen if I flopped.

The tight deadline ended up being a huge motivator for me. For the next two weeks I woke up early every morning to practice magic and the various stages of my performance. When my hands got too tired to continue training I spent hours per day introducing myself to people who were passing on the street, offering them free tickets (which had been provided by the club) to come see me work. I rehearsed things like my body positioning again and again so I would be able to impress the club owner with a tight 45 minute set. Nothing was perfect – there wasn't time for that – but my confidence grew and grew.

When the afternoon of the audition came I was pleasantly surprised to find that about four dozen attendees had shown up. Almost all of them fell into the category of "friends and family," something that still makes me feel gratitude for my loved ones to this day. The one person who *wasn't* in the room, though, was the club owner. I wanted to wait for him to arrive so I could be sure he didn't miss any of my dazzling illusions, but my patchwork audience started to grow impatient a few minutes after the starting time I had given. The show had to go on, so I got to work.

The actual magic act went well. I'm sure there would be a lot of little points I could critique if I saw that act again today, but it was a successful gig and the people who came to see it were entertained. I found out later that the club owner had dropped in for a few minutes and watched from the back of the room to see how things were going. He liked what he saw and gave me my own show. Just like that my career was on an upward trajectory.

The most important thing I took away from that two weeks wasn't about putting together a magic act, though. Instead, it was a reminder that nothing inspires us to action, or focuses our minds, quite as much as an impending deadline.

There is a reason procrastinating students suddenly become bookworms right before finals week. Many of you will know what it's like to finish an enormous amount of work right before a vacation. We all know how much more attention we pay to things like traffic lights when we're late for an important meeting.

In other words, it's easier to focus when we *have* to. That's what creating a sense of urgency is all about.

. . .

Cutting Away the Unnecessary

Another great thing about having urgency towards a big goal is that it doesn't just force you to move, but also to consider what is actually important at the moment.

Suppose I asked you to think about a classic question: if your home was on fire and you could only save three things, what would they be? Most of us don't like to think about losing everything in flames, but this dilemma gets repeated and discussed again and again because it forces us to consider what actually matters in our lives. If there was an immediate and pressing deadline, you would suddenly need to make decisions that kept you closer to what you love.

The same thing can happen with the dreams in your life. I could have easily put off performing when I arrived in New York City. I might have given my career more time to grow and take shape. I certainly could have studied with more instructors, got in extra practice, or invested more time in my image. Some teachers and mentors probably would have suggested I look for the ideal locations to work or checked out the pros and cons of various outfits, sound systems, and props.

That didn't happen, though, because I was pushed – in this case, by the Times Square club owner who put me on a tight deadline – to prepare and present my show. As a consequence I needed to figure out which pieces were going to be most important to my success. I couldn't sweat all the little details because I had to be prepared to get in front of an audience quickly.

That might sound stressful, but I think it was exactly what I needed at the time. In the years since then I have learned there isn't any such thing as a perfect speech or performance. As an entertainer you should always be getting better, but you'll never reach a point where every word and inflection are delivered just the right way or that audiences respond exactly how you would expect them to.

This is true in virtually any field or pursuit. You simply aren't going to be flawless. You are going to make bad decisions, do things the wrong way, and put yourselves on paths you have to retreat from later. But, it's far better to recognize that from the outset and get moving than it is to find yourself agonizing over little things that may turn out to be irrelevant later.

Some people are natural perfectionists because they can't stand to think about what will happen if things go wrong. Others use over preparation as a way to procrastinate. In either case, giving yourself a sense of urgency, even if it's from a deadline you've created in your own mind, can be a great solution. If you really want to be focused on a task or goal, you have to let go of the idea that you can control everything and simply keep pushing forward.

How Can You Create Urgency?

Often, we tend to think of urgency and pressing deadlines as constraints that are put upon us by the outside world. A supervisor, professor, or customer might ask for something in a hurry, for example, but most of us won't actually put the same kinds of pressure on ourselves. Why not?

If you want to be truly focused on an important task or goal, find a way to make it urgent. Take a first step, particularly if that step locks you into a further commitment.

For instance, you could pay to participate in an upcoming 5K road race, sign up for an open mic night, or fill out an application for an upcoming class. Each of these would turn your intention into something concrete, while also giving you a frame of time where you'd have to put up or shut up. In essence, you would be creating urgency by backing yourself into a corner. That can be scary, but it can also be exactly what's needed to get you moving if you feel like you're stuck in place.

Another way to create urgency is by making agreements you can't get out of. A classic example of this is finding a workout buddy who will go to the gym with you. If you know that person is going to show up at a certain time and don't want to disappoint them you'll make sure you are ready to hit the weights at that time, too.

You could rely on friends, family members, or even colleagues to make you accountable for a certain goal. Perhaps you owe them a few dollars every time you don't follow through on your promise, or you agree to buy lunches for week if you aren't able to finish a project by a certain deadline. The key in each of these cases is that there is just enough on the line to keep you concentrating on what you're trying to achieve and stop you from giving up when things get to be a little bit difficult. Strangely enough, the fear of letting others down can drive you to commit to your goals more than your worry about wasting your life. It's kind of like the way it's embarrassing to eat a big dessert in public but you can take down a whole pint of ice cream in half an hour on the couch at home (or at least that's what someone told me… I wouldn't know).

There are a lot of ways to build urgency, but I tend to think the bigger and more public something is, the better. When I performed my first magic show I knew my friends and family would be there. Also, if I didn't impress the club owner I knew I wouldn't be invited back again. The last thing I wanted was for things to go poorly.

Urgency forces action. It strips away your excuses, particularly if they revolve around fear, indecision, or a sense that things have to be perfect before you can go ahead. Find some way to impose a deadline on yourself or pay closer attention to the ones that are already in front of you. You might be amazed at what it does for your focus and work ethic.

Balancing Big Goals and Urgent Movement

Before I move away from this topic, I need to acknowledge an important piece of reality. When you set a big goal with a firm deadline in the name of creating urgency for yourself, it won't always work out perfectly. In fact, there are going to be times when you'll come up short. That's the risk you take for thinking big.

I would argue, though, that unless you have created a sense of urgency to do something like disarm a bomb or perform brain surgery, failure is not a terrible thing. Take it from someone with years and years of performing experience: there are worse things in the world than being defeated or embarrassed, even publicly. In fact, I would go so far as to say that the failures and setbacks you endure tend to be your biggest teachers.

I've had plenty of shows where there weren't as many audience members or volunteers as I might like. I know what it's like to be on stage and have things like speakers and lighting systems fail. I've missed flights and had my luggage end up in different time zones. Each of these was a hassle at the time, but they all made me much more resilient and better-prepared for the future.

Most of the time, when we think we have come up short what we've really done is learn something new and interesting. Or, we find out just how committed we are, and how much we actually want to achieve our most important goals.

None of this means you should ever plan for failure, of course, but I do want you to take away the important lesson that it's better to think big than it is to aim too small (for more on this, I recommend the book *The Magic of Thinking Big*). You want to be realistic, but not *too realistic*.

If you "create a sense of urgency" by promising yourself you'll earn a million dollars by next Tuesday it may feel like nothing more than a pipe dream if that amount of money feels unattainable to you. However, if you told everyone in your life that you'll have a million dollars five years from now it becomes the first step in a process. A tight deadline helps you focus, but an overwhelming one just distracts you from what you really want to accomplish.

Only you can find the right balance between setting a big and urgent goal and figuring out what can actually be accomplished from the point where you are, right now, in this moment. However, I would encourage you to stretch a little farther than is comfortable, and to dream a little bit bigger than your sense of realism allows. That way, even if you aren't able to achieve your goal right away you'll be on the path to doing something that feels truly amazing.

"Someday" Doesn't Always Come

Most of the things we want to get done in life aren't out of our reach; it's just that they never become urgent priorities. That fitness goal, the company we want to start, or the trip around the world we have been dying to take get put off, one day at a time, simply because they aren't urgent enough in the moment. There are other things that demand our focus and attention *right now*, even though they don't carry as much mental and emotional weight.

You can beat this tendency by creating your own urgency. Create a personal deadline and treat it with the same seriousness you would an assignment from your boss or professor. It won't be easy to put your own dreams and priorities first if you aren't used to doing so, but I can tell you from experience it's the difference between making coins disappear for kids and performing in Times Square.

Put yourself in a situation where you truly need to succeed and you might be amazed at what comes out of the process.

SEVEN

Take Care of Your Body

Looking into the mirror, I had to admit it: maybe I wasn't invincible after all.

This realization came to me as I was leaving a casino in Las Vegas, having lost a chunk of money I really needed. My wallet seemed to be getting slimmer every day, but the rest of me sure wasn't.

Just months before, I had been in the best shape of my life. Around that time a friend from high school moved to the town where I was living in Pennsylvania. I couldn't believe how great he looked. After a bit of catch up talk, he told me the story of how he'd gotten into bodybuilding. I'd put on a few pounds since my college days. It was like I had kept gaining the freshman 15 every year since graduation and seeing him made the contrast between what I was and what I should have been even worse. So, I asked if I could tag along to the gym.

He agreed, but it was clear he didn't expect me to actually follow through. I knew the feeling – after virtually every magic show or hypnosis performance, there are people wanting to know if I'll share a few tips or secrets with them. Most of the time, they ask a couple of questions and then quietly disappear when they realize how much work is involved in putting on a good show. Performing is a lot like exercising in that way. People love seeing the result, but they don't want to put in the effort it takes behind the scenes.

I *did* follow through, though. Whatever my friend did at the gym, I also did. When I saw him eating boiled chicken and broccoli, I did the same. I pestered him with questions until he gave me the advice I needed. In just a few months, I had shed more than 40 pounds and packed on some muscle. I was looking and feeling great.

Maybe it was the effect the fitness had on my self-confidence, but it was not long after that I decided to move to Las Vegas and pursue my passions of poker, magic, and hypnotism. Things got off to a great start. I found some part-time work and supplemented that by making a few thousand dollars every month at the tables.

There was only one problem. People like to say that Vegas never sleeps, and that's true. The stores and restaurants, however, *do* close at night. When I found myself leaving the casinos in the early morning hours I would grab fast food, or maybe some convenience store sweets, to satisfy my appetite. Before long my weight started creeping up again. Even worse, my mind had a hard time staying centered. All those unhealthy foods were messing with my brain chemistry. That wasn't just inconvenient, it was costing me money. My brain was getting fat while my wallet was getting thin.

I had to learn the hard way, as most of us do, that your mind can't function unless you take good care of your body.

The Mind Body Connection is Real

When you aren't feeling well physically you tend to be more tired and less focused. There are numerous reasons for this that involve brain chemistry, the nervous system, and other physiological details. I don't think we need to turn this chapter into a biology textbook that neither of us has the attention span for, though. That's because we've all had the feeling of being tired, sick, or even hungover. You already know how each of these conditions can stop you from concentrating or really paying attention to what you're doing.

In fact, when you're feeling under the weather that can be a distraction in and of itself. If you've got a cold or an infection, you're constantly being reminded by a headache or runny nose. It's difficult to make the most of your concentration under those circumstances.

Knowing all of this, if you're serious about getting focused and achieving your goals you have to make your health a priority. That's not to say you need to become someone who only sips green tea and eats organic vegetables (I certainly don't live that way), but you *do* have to be intentional about the way you treat your body. After all, it's going to influence your mind and your thoughts. If you suck at eating and get no rest, well then you're probably going to suck at thinking, too.

One of my mentors has taken this realization to an extreme level. He monitors his diet, consumes special herbs, and is careful to get plenty of sunshine every day. He also engages in regular yoga and meditation. You might not want to do those things, and you may think he's going overboard. But, when he explained his routine to me, he had a very simple rationale: to put himself in the right mental place to make multi-million dollar deals he needs to be as clear and relaxed as possible.

Whatever your individual healthy routine might look like – and health is something that can be different for every person – that's the kind of goal I think we should all aspire to. Imagine getting the daily food, rest, and exercise you need to think as clearly as you can. Envision what it would be like to feel completely calm, relaxed, and at ease in your work. What would that mean for your goals and your future?

As someone with ADHD, I'm keenly aware of the way my physical state affects my thinking. The wrong donut, soda, or coffee can turn me into the Tasmanian Devil. I guess it could be a burden, but I think of it as a positive. A lot of people aren't so conscious of the connection between what they do and eat and how it makes them feel. They undercut their own wellness and find it difficult to focus on what's in front of them, or what they're dealing with, because their bad eating and exercise habits feel harmless.

The connection between your mind and body is real

and it's immediate. Now let's get into a few of the ways you can move forward with that awareness.

To Focus Your Mind, Focus on Your Food

What you put into your body is largely going to dictate the way you feel. If you've been eating good, clean food, your thoughts are going to be clearer and sharper; if you stuff your stomach with junk, then you may discover you feel cloudy and irritable. Again, there is a science having to do with things like blood sugar and digestion at work.

It's easy to forget about these things, though, when you're craving a cheeseburger or a late-night snack. And certainly, there's nothing wrong with giving into temptation once in a while (remember what I said about willpower?) But, the big issue with bad food isn't just that it slows your body and your mind. Junk foods also tend to be addictive. When you eat a lot of salt and sugar, for instance, you start to crave even *more* salt and sugar. Then it gets harder and harder to focus, and you find yourself on a downward spiral that keeps you out of shape.

Like a lot of things in life, cleaning up your diet gets much easier with a little bit of planning and forethought. Just as you might take clothes to the dry cleaner or put gas in your car to plan for weekly meetings and commutes, try to get into the habit of planning your meals ahead. Don't leave your dietary decisions to the moment you're hungry. If you do, you'll almost inevitably end up eating the closest or most comforting highest-calorie item around. Ever wonder why so many people have the intention of eating salad but end the day with a face full of chocolate cake? That's the way your subconscious mind works – it wants whatever feels comforting after detecting a need.

By thinking about what you plan to have for the week, you can make healthier choices before they become snap decisions. You can also save time and money, particularly if you get used to preparing your own meals. And, like everything else I'm recommending, it's a habit. Once you start doing it, you'll realize how easy it is. Then, you'll begin to feel better, and that will cause you to keep going until you notice the benefits in your waistline and energy level. Before long, you won't have to think about it at all. You'll simply be the kind of person who eats well on a regular basis. You might not ever get addicted to kale, but you won't feel compelled to inhale junk food, either.

Deciding to "eat healthy" is a good start, but it isn't the end of the discussion. You also have to know your own body. As an easy example, most people will feel jittery with too much caffeine, leading to an inevitable crash. For someone with my type of ADHD, however, a cup of coffee can actually calm me down. I can also use caffeine to have a little more stamina during a workout, which can be beneficial when I'm trying to get the most out of my time in the gym.

You undoubtedly have your own quirks, preferences, and allergies. If you don't pay attention to your own body you can't take advantage of them. I recommend using a food journal for a couple of months. There are lots of apps out now that make it easy to start one, and for investing five or 10 minutes a day you can get a clearer picture of how your diet is affecting your moods and thoughts.

If you've never paid close attention to your diet before, you might be amazed at how a few changes in your eating can affect your ability to focus and stay motivated in a big way. If you want to reach for something big in life, you can start by reaching for the right things in your own refrigerator.

Rest and Healing are Critical to Focus

You can't expect to think clearly if you aren't getting enough rest. That's something we all know – both from advice and experience – but it's easy to ignore that knowledge when you feel like staying up late to spend some time with friends or just watch a movie.

Certainly, there are going to be occasions when skipping an hour or two in bed will be worth a drowsy morning, and sometimes a lack of sleep is unavoidable. I've taken a lot of redeye flights over the years to make it to a hypnosis show or a speaking engagement. The world doesn't end because I have an extra cup of coffee.

On the whole, though, it's important to get plenty of sleep if you want to focus your mind. New studies on the importance of rest are coming out all the time, but one of the things that's especially interesting is the way we reinforce learning through various sleep cycles.

In one Harvard research project, psychologists split students into two groups. Both were taught how to play a virtual-reality downhill skiing game. After the lesson one group was allowed to get the sleep they needed. The second group was woken and interrupted periodically. It's not surprising that the group that got sleep earned better scores over the course of the study. What *was* interesting, though, was the difficulty the sleepy students had in retaining what they learned.

This all lines up well with what we know about the role of rest on the brain. When your body is asleep, muscles are being repaired. At the same time, your subconscious mind is essentially working on the challenges and information it took on during the day. Your sleep is actually making you smarter. This occurs in both REM and non-REM cycles, which negates the popularly-held belief that you can get by with very little rest so long as you get a little bit of "deep sleep."

Even your dreams and nightmares, which can seem random and uncomfortable, are tied to the process of the subconscious storing and dealing with information. If you don't give your mind a chance to "catch up" with all it has seen and learned, you simply won't get smarter or more efficient.

The more you have to focus on the more crucial it is for you to get enough sleep. Of course, this runs contrary to what I see visiting college campuses regularly. At a time when young people should be absorbing the most information, and being best equipped to learn, far too many aren't getting enough rest for their minds to function properly.

You can't focus or pull the best out of yourself if you're walking around in a sleepy fog. If you haven't been making a solid night's rest a priority in your life before now, it's time to start thinking and behaving differently.

Ditch Stress to Calm Your Thoughts

Stress affects your ability to concentrate in a number of negative ways.

For one thing, when you have a lot of stress (which is essentially a persistent form of fear), it's difficult for your mind to focus on anything other than whatever you're worried about. It's the mental equivalent of a pebble in your shoe, continually bringing your attention back to an unresolved issue while you try to set your mind loose on something else.

Beyond that, stress affects your ability to rest and relax. It can destroy the quality of your sleep, leaving you feeling both fuzzy and depressed instead of sharp and energized. That's not going to help you think in an active or creative way.

Even if you were to get away from the effects of stress on your concentration there would also be lots of negative impacts on your health. Stress is linked with a number of diseases and ailments, especially over long periods of time. However, it's difficult to live a life that's free of worry, so how can you stop it from affecting your body and concentration?

The first step is to realize that some stress is healthier than others. If you feel a sense of internal pressure to always perform at your best, or to make the most from every day, that's not necessarily a bad thing. You don't want to lock yourself into a series of perfectionist tendencies that stop you from getting anything done, but it's okay to feel a little nudge to keep moving forward.

Another thing you can do is let go some of the stress you don't need. There are probably situations in your life you worry about but can't control. Suppose you find yourself lying awake and night and wondering whether an asteroid is going to impact the Earth. Unless you have a way of preventing that, you simply have to accept it as an unknown and move on.

You can also eliminate some of your stress by simply controlling your mental diet. Earlier, I advised you to think carefully about what you are putting into your body on a daily basis. Now it's time to do the same thing for your mind. For example, I stopped watching the news when I was a teenager. That might make me an irresponsible citizen, but also makes me a happier individual. There aren't many positive stories shown on nightly broadcasts and I don't want to start my day by seeing nothing but negative reporting. And I certainly won't benefit from putting all of that in my mind right before bed.

If you're used to consuming news, or low-quality programming that puts you in a bad mood, ask yourself this: wouldn't you rather have a nice conversation with your significant other to brighten your mood? What about keeping a journal of things you're grateful for, or reviewing your short and long-term goals? Any of these would help you to stay more focused on what matters and prevent you from taking on more stress you don't need. If something is truly important, you'll hear about it from scanning the headlines or listening to friends. There is a statement I love: "if it gets bad enough out there, someone will tell you." If it doesn't rise to that level you can trust that today's negative stories will just be replaced by others tomorrow.

Finally, we get to my favorite way to manage stress, and one that can solve a lot of your problems. That involves finding a form of exercise you enjoy and that relaxes you.

Using Fun Exercise to Strengthen Your Mind

You don't need me to tell you that exercise is good for you. You probably don't need me to point out that regular movement improves blood flow to your brain and the rest of your body, making it easier for you to stay energized and focused. What you might need is a better way of thinking about physical activity.

Far too many people treat exercise like a book report for their body. It's something they know they should do even though they would rather be watching TV or laying bed. I suspect that's because most people think of workouts in terms of what they imagine they should be doing, rather than a form of fitness they would enjoy.

For example, when you think about "getting in shape," what's the classic image? If you're like most people it's probably getting up at the crack of dawn to train for a marathon or some other endurance activity. That's great if you're the kind of person who naturally enjoys pounding the pavement, but what if you're somebody like me who *hates* the thought of putting in miles on a trail or treadmill? I'll take up running if and when I ever find myself being chased by a serial killer in clown makeup. Until then I'll pass.

How does someone stay fit with that kind of mindset? The answer is to stop thinking about exercise like an either/or choice. The decision isn't between pursuing a hobby that feels like a chore or watching your health decline. You can find something that suits your interests and body type. You'll have more fun and might actually look forward to working out.

For my part, I have a few sports I enjoy but especially love the time I take training in mixed martial arts. While running is a solitary activity that leaves me alone with too many thoughts, in an MMA class I can interact with other people and participate in lots of fun drills that change every few minutes. I get a chance to really enjoy myself while learning something new and increasing my fitness.

You might like volleyball, tennis, golf, weightlifting, or something else. Maybe you just want to pay a few neighborhood kids a couple of dollars and throw dodgeballs at them for 15 minutes. Why not? It might not be the "perfect" fitness routine, but it's better than doing nothing and if you truly enjoy it, you'll keep up with your habit over time.

Like all the other healthy habits I'm advocating, exercise can actually become a little bit addictive over time. You simply become the kind of person who works out so it doesn't take any effort to keep going. That's especially true when your body starts to produce endorphins and you discover the feeling I call "good tired."

This occurs when you've had a grueling session that leaves you a little bit sore, but in a pleasant way. Your mind is completely still, and you feel great about yourself because you've accomplished something and focused your brain on an immediate task rather than all the little stressors that can pile up in day-to-day life.

When I'm rolling on the mat with a training partner who would love to choke me out or force me into a hold I can't escape from, there simply isn't room to be concerned about a client I need to call or a bill I'll eventually have to pay. My mind will return to these things later, of course, but only after I've turned those worries off completely for a couple of hours and decreased my stress. I'll be able to approach them from a calmer, more positive perspective. That's the power of good tired.

The hard part about any exercise routine is simply getting started. In the beginning, you're going to have to draw a little bit of that willpower I mentioned before. That's what it's there for – to get you started on positive projects, not to push you to keep doing things you don't enjoy.

Here's my advice to you: if you aren't currently getting enough (or any) exercise, literally put this book down right now and get started. Try an activity you think you might like for 15 or 20 minutes. If you find you really enjoy it, do it again tomorrow or the next day. If not, try something else.

Just take that step and you'll be amazed at how much better you'll start to feel. Right away you'll get a burst of energy and enthusiasm from having done something to better yourself. Before long, you'll start to get relief in the form of healthier weight control and better overall health. You'll feel clear and energetic. Those shots of dopamine will start flying into your brain with every completed workout and you'll begin each day feeling stronger and more confident. It's a domino effect of positivity that can keep paying off for the rest of your life.

Focus Has a Physical Component

I hope I've convinced you how important it is to take care of your body. When you're eating right, getting plenty of rest, and managing stress with positivity and exercise it feels possible to overcome any challenge. When you aren't doing these things it's difficult to remain focused on what's right in front of you, much less any long-term goals.

In the early days of psychology, some researchers speculated that the mind and body were entirely separate entities. Now we know better. If you want your mind running like a well-tuned engine, make things easier by taking care of your body first.

EIGHT

Use Meditation and Mindfulness

I'll always remember the first time I sat down to meditate. Following the careful instruction of my patient guru, I folded my body into a lotus pose and began to breathe gently. Each movement of air in and out of my lungs became more serene and deliberate. Soon, reality itself seemed to fade away until there was only a sense of warmth, awareness, and love for all creatures.

Or at least that's how I imagined it.

In the real world, several minutes went by while I tried desperately to push away unwanted thoughts and physical sensations. You'll never know how many random ideas are floating around in your brain, and how many different ways your nose can itch, until you actively try to ignore them.

The truth is I didn't really get anything out of my first few attempts at mindfulness. But, I kept at it. I continued to try meditating just as I stuck with my fitness plan when it was hard, or the way I refused to give up on magic tricks I was struggling to learn. With enough effort, the impossible became easy.

There isn't any surprise in this, of course. Everything in life gets easier with practice. That's something I want you to remember as we approach the subject of meditation and mindfulness. Both can have wonderful effects on your life for a number of reasons, and each one gives you a chance to effectively "practice" a state of pure concentration. Work with them often enough and you'll develop the kind of mindset that can stay locked in on one important task or idea at a time. Those benefits might not come immediately, though, and it's easy to get frustrated while you're learning.

The frustration pays off. Practicing meditation, mindfulness, and self-hypnosis is a good way to clear away distractions and anxiety. I often find that my mind is like a rabbit. Sometimes, it can run and zigzag from one topic or idea to the next. But when I get it calmed down it can sit – fluffy and content – until more activity is needed. That's the power of being intentional about your thinking, and I'm going to show you how you can use it to improve your focus, reach your goals, and improve your life.

But first, let's get an important detail out of the way…

What You Call it Doesn't Matter

In this chapter I'm going to introduce you to my favorite methods of mediation and self-hypnosis. Some people would call these by the same names I use. Others might think of them as relaxation, clearing your head, refocusing, or just being mindful. In truth, there are only minor differences between the definitions. Psychologists can argue about what makes something more meditative than hypnotic, but it doesn't really matter for our purposes. You can refer to it as turning into a pod person for all I care. What's important is that these techniques work.

So, I don't want you to get hung up on labels or worry that anything I suggest is going to turn you into a literal zombie. As much fun as that might be, what we are going to accomplish is quite the opposite. We're going to sharpen your focus to the point where your mind feels clear, light, and creative. When that happens, it doesn't really matter what you call the process.

Another thing that should be noted is that these techniques all go back generations. They've been known to scholars and thinkers, not to mention shamans and priests, for hundreds and thousands of years. In some cases, they've been associated with different groups or movements, but that isn't because they are inherently mystical. Instead, they are based on simple human psychology. Our brains are built for hyperfocusing. It doesn't take any special faith or controlled substance to unlock this part of your mental potential.

With that disclaimer out of the way, I'm hoping you feel comfortable enough to give these methods a try. Start experimenting with them and you may be amazed at how you can direct your mind towards what's important to you and away from distractions that might've been holding you back.

. . .

Slowing Your Mind with Meditation

Your mind is like a car. It has several different gears and speeds, each appropriate for certain situations. Psychologists have names for different brainwave states (Alpha, Theta, Delta, etc.), but you don't have to know the science to understand the bigger truth. After all, you recognize intuitively that it feels much different to be excited and have your thoughts coming faster than you can handle them than it does to be content, relaxed, and on the edge of sleep.

Having a rapid pattern of thoughts can be beneficial if you are stressed or threatened. It's a natural response to potentially dangerous situations. One problem with our modern world, though, is that we encounter all kinds of stimuli that *feel* like they are urgent and stressful even if they shouldn't be. Ringing phones, email interruptions, and traffic noises are all examples of triggers that affect us subconsciously even when they aren't important to our immediate safety. Add in deadlines or multitasking priorities and it's easy to see why we can feel overwhelmed even when it seems like "nothing is happening."

Meditation, or simple mindfulness, gives you a simple way to turn down the noise in your mind. It's extraordinarily helpful for those of us with ADHD, of course, but it can be beneficial for anyone. It's all about clearing your mind, taking unnecessary thoughts away, and giving yourself a beautiful sense of relaxation. That's great for relieving stress, but it also lets you focus more sharply. It's like taking a break between workouts. When you replenish your mental strength you can come back better than you were before you had a rest.

There are a number of different ways to meditate, of course, and I would encourage you to practice, experiment, and find the methods that are most relaxing to you. For the purposes of getting you started, though, I'm going to share with you one of my favorite techniques. It's quick, simple, and effective for lots of people. It can brighten your day in just a few minutes and will leave you feeling calm and clear. Let's see how it works:

Light a candle and place it a couple of feet in front of you (preferably in a place where there isn't any risk it will burn down your home or work).

Sit comfortably. Fix your eyes on the candle and take a few deep breaths. Ease out any tension you might have in your head, your neck, or your shoulders.

Continue to keep your gaze fixed on the candle while you allow your breaths to get deeper and deeper. If thoughts enter your mind, think of them floating away like clouds. Just keep breathing and staring at the flame. Just watch it dance and follow its movements. Allow yourself to concentrate on it without worrying about anything that was on your mind before you started.

I'm going to pause here for second and let you know that this single technique, if practiced for just a few minutes a day, can improve your mood and concentration immensely. Most of us don't get (or take) the time we should to actually clear our minds. Simply bringing your attention to your breath, and fixating on a simple flame, can help you gain energy and perspective. Just set a timer for a few minutes and stop when you reach your goal. You'll be amazed at how much better you feel.

However, if you want to get the most from your meditation, you can add a couple of steps.

First, keep gazing at the flame until your eyes feel heavy. If at some point you feel relaxed enough, allow them to close while you continue to breathe deeply.

Once this happens, repeat a mantra you have established for yourself in your mind. Make it something short, positive, and present-tense. Here are a couple of good examples:

"I am more calm, confident, and relaxed every day."

"I am enjoying life more and more as I reach my goals."

"I enjoy the life I have created."

"I am focused on my most important goal, which is ____."

"I am healthy and energetic."

These are just examples, but they illustrate a point. By repeating a mantra you stay focused on something positive that matters to you while simultaneously pushing away unnecessary thoughts.

Note that each of these statements is expressed in the first-person present tense. "I am a non-smoker" or "I make a million dollars" is better than "I will quit smoking" or "I am going to make a million dollars." That's because your subconscious will consider a future statement as something that can happen someday, but not necessarily now. By focusing on the present, you force it to look for solutions and connections that make a different "right now".

Continue repeating your mantra, either in your mind or out loud, until your time is up. Then you can shift your focus back to wherever it needs to be for the next part of your day.

When practicing mindfulness, don't worry that you aren't "doing it right" or that you get distracted by an outside noise. You'll get better as you go along, and you may find that you enter a flow state quite easily.

In his book *Stealing Fire* author Steve Kotler shares how he practiced meditation regularly while having researchers study his brain waves and breathing patterns. In just a few weekends he was able to nearly duplicate the physical signs displayed by Buddhist monks. It's easier than you think to clear your mind if you're willing to practice, and the benefits are bigger than you might imagine.

Entering a Self-Hypnotic State

When I'm booked to do a speech or comedy hypnosis show, people show up to see me hypnotize their friends or coworkers. That's the simplest explanation for all of the fun and amazing things that happen on stage, but it's probably more accurate to say that I help my participants to enter a state of hypnosis on their own. In other words, it's something they do to themselves; I just guide them along.

That's important to know because once you understand that virtually all hypnosis is self-hypnosis, you start to see how easy it is to put yourself in a trance state. In fact, you probably do it all the time already. You "zone out" while watching television, playing video games, or driving on a highway. The only difference between that sort of occurrence and the process I'm going to lay out is intention. When you enter a hypnotic state by accident you simply relax. I'm going to show you how to use the same dynamic to increase your powers of concentration and motivation.

The process of hypnotizing yourself and giving suggestions is very similar to the one I outlined for being mindful. It just essentially takes the exercise one step further. Once again, it's simple, safe, and completely free. So, let's look at how you do it step-by-step:

Sit in a comfortable place and position. You may want to set a timer or phone reminder so you won't have to worry about losing track of the minutes.

Take a deep breath and close your eyes. After a moment, imagine there is a calm and silent person beginning to massage your head and neck.

(Don't worry. It doesn't matter what this person looks like or who they are. It isn't *that* kind of massage).

Envision that person massaging your shoulders, your back, your legs, and even down to your toes. Imagine that as they do, a sense of warmth comes over your body. Feel yourself becoming completely relaxed as you breathe more and more deeply.

Once you feel your mind is still enough that all your thoughts and worries are draining away, begin to introduce suggestions, just like we did before. This time, though, we're going to be more intentional about the messages you give your deeper mind. In particular, you want the suggestions to be positive, present-tense, and self-affirming.

Here are few self-hypnotic suggestions you can use or adapt to your own situation…

"I am a confident and energetic person who is getting stronger every day."

"I weigh 150 pounds because I eat healthy foods and get plenty of exercise."

"I am successful in my career and am earning $100,000 per year."

Again, these are only sample statements. They may or may not reflect your own goals. However, the point remains that no matter what your specific affirmations look like, you are going through the process of clearing your mind. Then, once you're relaxed, you are replacing existing thoughts with others that bring you closer to the life you want to live.

Continue with your suggestions until your time has finished. Then, gently allow yourself to return your consciousness to the present moment until you feel fully awake and alert.

This basic self-hypnosis framework has been used by millions of people, including some of the world's most focused and successful individuals. In my experience, high achievers tend to be very good hypnotic subjects. They've usually been visualizing their own success for many years. Think of an Olympic skier. That kind of person doesn't just go out and perform. Instead, they constantly go through runs and courses in their minds, mentally perfecting them again and again.

Every person is different, and we don't all respond to the same hypnotic prompts or inductions. With that in mind, I want to offer you a couple of variations you may find useful.

The first is to substitute a mental massage for the visual countdown. That is, you can begin with the number 10 and go to 9 while consciously breathing deeply and letting go of all the tension in your forehead and eyes. Then, while moving from 9 to 8, release the muscles in your jaw. Continue counting down while you relax your neck, your back, etc., and let that sensation of warmth run through your body. Some people find it easier to work from fixed numerals than they do a visualized massage.

Another technique to keep yourself focused is to enter a state of self-hypnosis with the aid of a recording. If you'd like, you can use a clip where you guide yourself through the exercises I've already outlined. Or, you can visit my website (ericmina.com) and use one of the recordings I provide. That way, your hypnosis session will be guided from start to finish.

Once again, I want to point out that hypnotizing yourself won't make you a zombie. Neither are you likely to find that you'll enter a deep trance immediately. With a bit of time and practice, however, you can use these techniques to clear your mind. Even more importantly, you can use them to change your habits and thought patterns so you feel sharper, clearer, and more motivated.

All that's left at that point is to incorporate mindfulness and self-hypnosis into your daily routine.

Being Mindful Throughout the Day

Practicing mindfulness is like working out or balancing your checkbook – you'll get a much greater benefit from doing it at regular brief intervals then you will trying to become a Zen master all at once. You might be amazed at what a few short breaks each day will do for you, even if they only last five minutes each.

Personally, I try to set up my schedule so that I can stop what I'm doing at least a few times a day and calm my mind. I do this partly for the enjoyment, but also because it helps me to stay sharp and focused as I move from one role, task, or activity to the next.

For instance, I might decide to take a five-minute meditation break late in the morning, and then practice self-hypnosis for 10 minutes using a recording before my evening starts. I also like to pause what I'm doing occasionally to look at my vision boards. These are simply pages or posters I have put together that remind me of my most important targets in life.

For example, my first vision board has all my big dreams and goals summed up. It reminds me of the amount of money I'd like to have, the type of career I aspire to, and what I would look and feel like in peak physical condition. Just glancing at this from time to time reminds me of what I'm working for and it helps me to keep my priorities straight.

My second vision board is more immediate. It might have short-term financial goals, for instance, or a reminder to finish an upcoming project. I try to keep this one somewhere in my field of vision at all times so I'm constantly being brought back to whatever it is I'm working on in a particular moment.

If this sounds excessive, just remember how easy it is to get distracted from something that's truly important in your life. It only takes a moment to be pulled away by your phone, or a something that's happening on the other side of a door or window. Once that happens, the momentum you were making towards an important life goal – like retiring comfortably or getting into great shape – is put in jeopardy.

Learning experts say the easiest way to master a new language is to be immersed in it. If you wanted to speak Spanish fluently, it would make sense to surround yourself with people who only spoke Spanish until you picked up every accent and intonation. In a rather short period of time you would actually begin to *think* in your new tongue.

It's largely the same way with focus. If you want to stay sharp, mindful, and relaxed, you need to set up your day in a way that encourages that goal. You want to be immersed in your own motivation. Do that and you can benefit from reminding yourself to concentrate on the things that are important to you rather than the ones that are simply easiest to pay attention to when you're feeling tired or bored.

Meditation, mindfulness, and self-hypnosis can help you to literally strengthen your powers of concentration and achieve more every day. But, you have to be intentional about the way you use them and keep practicing until the benefits become clear.

NINE

Give Your Mind a Break

For much of this book, I've advised you to find ways to keep pushing yourself so you won't be distracted or pulled away from your most important goals, projects, and priorities. However, my last tip on building a more focused life is to make sure you throw the rules out the window once in a while. Sometimes you just have to take a break, cut loose, and do things that make you feel good.

This can be a hard thing to do, particularly when you're pushing ahead and generating momentum towards a target that's important to you. It's nice watching the money roll in, and seeing extra weight come off can feel fantastic. It can be so good that you don't want to enjoy an afternoon off or take a cheat day even though you know you're pushing too hard. However, we all need regular rest and relaxation, not to mention the occasional change of pace. If we never took a pause we would get ground down very quickly.

Great thinkers throughout history have recognized

this. David Thoreau, Mark Twain, and Anthony Bourdain were just a few of the authors who showed that we open up a world outside ourselves, and feel calmer within, when we take the time to break away from our normal routines and thought patterns. I think their advice is especially relevant now, when we all seem to be "on" at all times and distracted so frequently. Just having a bit of peace and quiet can mean a lot.

This isn't just an idle concept to me. To me, getting the occasional break, in the form of a vacation, an afternoon off, or even a cheat day from my nutritional plan, is a bit like turning off the motor in my brain so it can cool down. It just means I will be that much fresher and more prepared in the future.

I enjoy what I do for work, but it can be great to see an empty week on my schedule. Sometimes, after I've been out on the road for weeks giving speeches and hypnosis shows, I come back home and do absolutely nothing for a few days. Even though part of me might feel like I should be talking to meeting planners, writing new articles, or otherwise promoting myself to meeting planners, years of experience have taught me that I need to relax until I'm ready to jump back in with all of my energy and enthusiasm. Otherwise, I'll just end up paying for it later.

That brings me to the first thing you have to remember about giving yourself a break if you want to stay focused and engaged…

Too Much of Anything Hurts

No matter how positive something in your life is, there is a risk that comes with overdoing it. Too much of anything can hurt you.

For an obvious example, you only have to look at the way we build and maintain physical fitness. Generally speaking, the problem most people have when trying to get into shape is they simply don't eat right or exercise enough. Hang out in a gym for a while, though, and you'll learn that there are a whole lot of people who can't make further gains on their strength or endurance because they are actually training *too much.* Their bodies get worn out and their muscles can't respond and rebuild.

While that concept might seem unimaginable to someone who is just looking to lose a little bit of weight, it's a common enough problem that coaches and trainers know to look out for the signs.

The same goes for virtually anything else you do. Focus too hard on a single point or idea and you'll lose sight of the context that made it important in the first place. Study too long and your mind will cease to absorb information. Spend so much time working without a vacation and you'll stop being effective at your job.

Obviously, physical and mental fatigue are important parts of this equation, but so is motivation. When you do too much of anything – even something you love – you can get tired of it. At that point, your joy or appreciation for the activity can fade away. After that you're simply left with a routine you're sticking to for no discernible reason, or a job you stay in because it's comfortable. That's not going to help you keep your mind focused, and it's certainly not going to make you happy.

It's easy, once you sharpen your powers of focus, to take on a kind of single-minded determination. That's a good thing, but you don't want to push it too hard. Make room in your life for the people, hobbies, and routines that keep you healthy and refreshed. That could mean slowing down progress towards your goals in the short term, but it's going to keep you moving in the right direction over the long run.

Earlier in this book I advised you to do more of what you enjoy. Maybe a good add-on to that rule would be to avoid turning your favorite activities into a chore. It's easier to do than you might imagine, particularly if you aren't maintaining your own mental and physical health by taking time out to recover.

Rest and Relaxation Are About Growth

I want to stick with the theme of physical training for the moment because there is a popular misconception that the time you spend in the gym builds muscle. Believe it or not, that idea isn't technically correct. When you work out, you're tearing muscle down so it can be rebuilt later. You're getting stronger when you rest and the body repairs, even though you don't notice it while it happens.

The same thing applies to sleep. Although psychologists are still learning a lot about the time we spend unconscious in our beds, there is a general consensus that patterns and observations are reinforced while we rest. In other words, we literally get smarter and absorb our experiences when we sleep. Staying up all night to study or work on a project might seem ambitious, but it's not that different from walking into a bar and putting a bunch of drinks on a credit card. There could be a short-term payoff, but you'll pay more for the splurge later when you go through a hangover and get your bill in the mail.

Of course, "getting rest" doesn't just mean sitting on the couch after you've had a rotten day or watching TV following a long day in the classroom or office. Or at least it shouldn't *always* mean that. The most beneficial kinds of downtime involve having fun, learning new skills, and strengthening social bonds. So, the time you spend in bed or vegging out in front of the tube is fine, but make sure you mix in a walk with your significant other, a few minutes spent gardening, or even a volunteer session for a local charity. As counterproductive as it might seem, when you are focused on reaching a specific outcome, it could be the best thing for your focus and state of mind.

There's an old parable about two lumberjacks who decide to have a contest to see who can cut more wood over the course of the day. The first starts excitedly, hammering away with all of his might for hours on end. The second works methodically, occasionally sitting down and stopping altogether.

When the contest is ended the two men compare piles of lumber. The first lumberjack is amazed to find he has cut fewer trees than his competitor. Angry and confused, he accuses the other man of cheating. "I worked harder," he says. "There isn't any way you could have beaten me while you took all those breaks."

The second lumberjack's explanation? "Every time I took a break I sharpened my axe."

That sums up the importance of rest and relaxation perfectly. If you never allow your mind to get dull you can continue focusing on things that are important on a day-to-day basis. Then, even though it might look and feel like you aren't pushing as hard as you could be, you will be able to stay a step ahead of everyone else who lacks the same kind of perspective.

Make the Most of Small Pauses

Everyone has their own idea of what rest and rejuvenation should look like, but I want to point out that there are at least a couple of ways you should give yourself a regular break. One has to do with your daily and weekly habits, and the other involves your longer-term plans.

In terms of your day-to-day routine, I strongly advise you build little breaks into your schedule. For instance, promise yourself you'll be focused, present, and engaged in what you're working on for couple of hours, but then you'll give yourself a break to check social media or watch some viral videos. Your break could be chatting with a coworker over a cup of coffee or taking a walk around the block. It could even be slapping yourself in the face with a rubber chicken if that's what you're into.

What matters here is that you don't become so

intense or locked in that you get burnt out. The harder you work on becoming a focused person the sharper your attention span will get, but unless you are completely engrossed in what you're doing you should remember to step away for at least a few minutes.

I like to combine this idea with some of my other mindfulness practices. For instance, I make it a habit to meditate for a few minutes in the morning, and to schedule little breaks where I'll go and stare at my vision board. These small pauses serve a dual purpose. On the one hand they get me away from something I might have been thinking too narrowly about. And on the other, they just reinforce my bigger sense of focus by reminding me of my most important goals.

You could certainly do something similar with very little effort. It's much easier to stay on task when you know your next break and reward is around the corner. Also, it's never a bad thing to keep stoking your drive and motivation.

It's easy to convince yourself that you're too busy to ever take a break from what you're doing. That's hardly ever the case, though. I hate to say it, but most of us aren't nearly as important or crucial to the functioning of the world as we would like to think. And even those who are (like police officers or air traffic controllers) have others who can cover for them for a few minutes at a time.

Remember that these little breaks don't have to be a big deal, and you can incorporate them into your schedule in any way that makes sense. What is important is you have the understanding that your mind can't run for hours and hours on end without any kind of rest under normal circumstances. However, if you can use a few minutes of your time to get refreshed – and even better, concentrate on your goals – you will find your ability to stay focused goes a lot farther than you imagined.

Perspective Comes From Distance

I mentioned there are two important aspects to building regular breaks into your life. The first has to do with building small interruptions into your daily schedule. The second is making time to get away from your normal routine.

Ideally, this would involve both physical and emotional distance. There are big benefits that come with traveling. You get exposed to new cultures and ideas, of course, but you also get the chance to think about your own life and routines without being immersed in them. You get space to think about who you really are, what you really want, and how the various pieces of your life fit together. You'll see situations, career plans, and even relationships in a whole new light.

I couldn't tell you how many times I have come upon some sort of breakthrough at a moment when I wasn't actively thinking about a certain problem or challenge. Instead, I was walking on a beach, sitting on an airplane, or hiking far from home. You have undoubtedly had the same experience.

There is a scientific explanation for this. Our

subconscious minds – the same parts of our brain we tap into with hypnosis – don't let go of our struggles just because we stop consciously focusing on them. However, our neurons can get stuck in certain grooves. By getting away from those, and seeing, hearing, or tasting new things, we can snap out of old patterns. We relax and distract ourselves while giving our unconscious a chance to try out new answers and connections.

If you were to take your hand and hold it an inch from your face you wouldn't see anything but vague impressions of the color and lines. Extend your arm, though, and other details come into focus. That's the way we need to treat our problems and challenges sometimes. Just as our bodies and minds are connected, our thoughts and thought patterns are heavily influenced by our surroundings at any given moment.

Take advantage of the opportunities you have to get some physical, mental, and emotional distance from your everyday life once in a while. You might be surprised at what you see once you look at your life from a different perspective.

What Do You Really Want?

Having regular breaks – especially the kinds of big ones that shift your entire focus on life thinking – can be beneficial in one more way by helping you to narrow in on the right direction.

Earlier in this book, I advised you to pay attention to the goals and dreams that actually move you to do something about them. The ones that excite you are the most motivating and can make the biggest difference in your life. What truly matters to you at one point, however, may not match your biggest dreams and priorities later. If you aren't careful, you can gradually find yourself chasing goals that don't mean a whole lot.

However, when you're able to break away from your everyday habits you get the chance to think about things differently. In fact, this might occur even if you aren't "thinking" about things at all. In the same way that your subconscious can come up with new solutions when you're relaxed or engaged in something else, it can also help you to be thoughtful and reflective.

To give a sense of how you can use this in your own life, set aside a few hours towards the end of your next vacation to make some lists. Write out the things that are important to you, the goals you'd like to meet over the next year, or the worries that have been troubling you. Assuming you've been away from home for at least a few days, you might find that some of the thoughts that come to you are a little bit surprising. That's completely normal. It just means your unconscious is getting the opportunity to sort things and put them in their proper places without the pressure of meeting deadlines and dealing with day-to-day distractions.

What you want from your life is going to change in some ways whether you want it to or not. By taking regular breaks you get the opportunity to "check in" with yourself so you don't spend all your time and energy chasing a goal that has lost its meaning along the way.

TEN

Going from Blurry to Brilliant

I'm a lucky guy. My life makes me happy. I get to fly around from city to city entertaining people and teaching them about the power of their own minds. I feel like that's not too bad for somebody who struggled to get through every level of school and was told by more than one teacher he would probably end up working in fast food. The fact that I did it without medication just makes it sweeter for me… and proves it's possible for you, too.

Turning the hard (and sometimes strange) lessons of my life into something you can use is what this book is all about. In this final chapter I want to do two things. First, I want to give you one last word of encouragement. Whatever it is you're going through, or whatever challenges might be in front of you, you can beat them. While it's true that we live in a world that is literally working against our powers of focus, motivation, and concentration, you can come out on top. Everything you need is inside of you. Remember: you are the superhero of your own story

The second thing I want to do is give you a quick set of tips and reminders you can use to keep moving ahead, particularly when things feel tough or hopeless. I want this to be a chapter you could come back to again and again and read in a few minutes when you need a nudge that pushes you back towards your amazing self.

If you haven't read the parts of the book that came before this, I hope you'll go back and peek at them now. I really didn't write all that much, so it shouldn't take hours and hours to get through each chapter. And, the advice you'll find could transform your life – I know it's certainly done wonders for mine.

With that caveat out of the way, let's look at the quick set of tips I hope you'll remember as you make your own journey from blurry to brilliant.

Find What You Love

The one thing that is absolutely irreplaceable in your life is passion. There's simply no substitute for getting out of bed in the morning and being jazzed about what the future holds for you.

You probably aren't going to be excited about every moment of every day, or look forward to all the responsibilities you have to face. However, what you can do is choose a path that lifts and inspires you. Then, once you're working in that direction you can set up your life in a way that means dealing with fewer hassles and stressors.

One of the perks of my job is that I get to meet a lot of successful and interesting people. I've found that it's very, very unusual to find someone who is at the top of their field and isn't enjoying their profession. And even if they don't enjoy what they are doing they just enjoy winning. That's true in sports, entertainment, academia, and every aspect of the business world. It's so much easier to get ahead when you have a sense of joy about where you're going.

If you need to make changes in your life, understand that it's all right if you can't follow up on them instantly. Over time, though, you should absolutely try to find what you love and make that a big part of your work and purpose. When it comes to finding the way forward, never forget the *why* is more important than the *how*.

Don't Expect Everything to Happen at Once

You might remember I happen to really love movies. However, I think there is a downside to watching too many of them. They tend to reduce conflict, struggle, and hard work down to back stories and quick montages.

This is true even in my book. While I've highlighted some of the setbacks I've faced, I'm guessing it's going to be easier for you to read about my defeats than it was for me to live through them. Believe me when I tell you some of them weren't as entertaining in real time. They have helped me become who I am, and I'm grateful for the resilience they taught me, but that doesn't mean I enjoyed every minute or that my path to becoming a well-known speaker, hypnotist, and magician was a smooth one.

The point I want to make here is that you shouldn't expect everything to happen for you all at once. Life isn't like the movies. There are going to be ups and downs, particularly if you're trying to make hard changes or improvements. Later, you'll look back on the struggle with a sense of joy and accomplishment. In the meantime you just have to keep persevering in the face of adversity.

Remember That Success is About Habits

Often, when we look back on our biggest triumphs we tend to think of crowning achievements and standout moments. It's the race we won, the award we received, or (in my case) the standing ovation that followed a successful presentation.

What's easy to forget is that these moments don't come out of nowhere. In almost every case they are made possible by the hard work that gets done before we break through. In other words, it is the small habits we pursue on a daily basis that put us over the top, not any single effort or stroke of luck.

You may have heard this riddle before, but it's highly relevant to the point I want to make: a worker is tasked with breaking a boulder down to smaller parts. So, he finds a sledgehammer and starts striking the giant rock, one blow after another, over the course of many days. Finally, after so many thousands of attempts that he's lost count, the stone shatters into smaller pieces. Was that the result of one particularly strong swing, or the cumulative effect of the gradual effort? Anyone who understands the natural course of things will know that this triumph, like most, results from persistence rather than strength.

If you go back through history all the way to thinkers like Plato and Marcus Aurelius, you'll find that the power of maintaining consistent habits has been an ingredient of success for centuries. The person who gets up just a little bit earlier, stays a little longer, or keeps their mind focused on the task at hand a little bit better will eventually end up on top.

Nothing I've recommended in this book requires you to make huge and immediate shifts in your life or schedule. That's intentional. Not only would most people fail to follow through on such big commitments, but becoming the person you've always wanted to be is about accumulating small habits on a day-to-day basis rather than making overnight transformations.

Take Care of Yourself

Common sense will tell you that your mind and body perform their best when you're taking care of them. You wouldn't decide to drive thousands of miles without ever checking the oil and tires on your car, so why embark in a brand-new direction without putting together a plan for your own health and fitness?

I hope you'll keep that analogy in mind as you put some of the ideas in this book to use. In our culture there is a tendency to overlook self-care. In fact, many people admire those who seem to be driven to the point of becoming workaholics. However, the "first-in, last-out" mindset has limits. Neglecting your own physical and emotional needs can take you straight to burnout rather than carrying you to achievement.

I want you to stay driven and seek out the success you deserve. As you do, though, put just as much importance on things like rest, relaxation, and time away as you do the other habits that keep you focused. You can't concentrate if your mind is tired, and you'll have a hard time making steady progress toward your dreams if you continually feel like you're on the edge of exhaustion.

You do most of your growing and strengthening when you're resting, not working. Remember to keep sharpening that axe and give yourself the room you need to keep getting better each and every day.

Keep Learning and Strengthening Your Mind

One thing that seems to surprise people is that I read a lot. They tend to assume that having ADHD means I can't focus on a book, but that's not quite right – I have no trouble keeping my mind on things I'm interested in. I use that to my advantage by always feeding my brain new ideas on the topics I write about, speak about, and think about. You can do the same thing and become better at the things you're passionate about as a result.

Picking up new knowledge lets you essentially skip ahead in line when it comes to gaining skills and perspectives. Think about this way: when you read a book like this one you can absorb everything an expert has learned on a particular subject in just a couple of hours. That's amazing! It took me decades to come up with a plan to manage my focus, and nearly a year to organize those thoughts into the words you're reading right now. You don't have to go through the same process to learn what I know – you just have to spend some time reading it.

I would definitely encourage you to come back and revisit these chapters again as you need them, or as they become more relevant to your life. However, I also hope you'll pick up books, videos, and other materials by experts on productivity, time management, motivation, and any other topics that will help you to reach your dreams. I fell in love with reading and it has made all the difference in my life. It can help you to grow, too.

The world always needs people who are more informed, and the upside of the digital age is that everything you want to know is available at your fingertips.

Don't Be Afraid to Jump

At numerous points in my life I ran into situations where I had the choice to do the "smart" thing and prepare or simply jump in with both feet and see what would happen. More often than not I chose the second option. It usually worked.

There is a lot of value in getting to know the details of any plan or project. But, there is also a risk in knowing *too much*. Not only is experience the best teacher, but if you study anything long enough you could become overloaded with different perspectives or ideas. In other words, too much information can lead you to paralysis.

When you're faced with a big choice about whether to take action or not, ask yourself this: what is the worst thing that could happen if you come up short? Unless you're facing death, financial ruin, or the loss of a cornerstone relationship in your life, it's probably worth it to just take the chance. Things like embarrassment fade very quickly and you are more likely to succeed than you realize.

Most of us underestimate our own capabilities and overestimate the amount of time and preparation we need to pull off something big. Don't be afraid to jump forward if it will bring you one step closer to the life you really want.

Give Yourself a Break

In my experience, procrastination is probably the biggest obstacle to change that most people face. They assume there will always be time to chase their dreams or get serious about their next step forward, even though life moves faster than they realize.

The second biggest problem, though, is that many of us tend to be way too hard on ourselves when we aren't as successful as we would like. We take it as a sign that we should give up, that we aren't good enough, or that we aren't destined for bigger things. We compare our efforts to what we see on Facebook and YouTube, which leaves us mistakenly thinking that we will never measure up or get where we want to go.

Don't compare your chapter 1 to someone else's chapter 10.

If you ever catch yourself feeling that way, simply decide to give yourself a break. For one thing, we are all born with different skills, talents, and advantages. You don't necessarily have to be the best at your job or hobby. And for another, being good at anything is usually a function of practice, focus, and determination. Don't let a setback become a stopping point.

Should it happen that you can't or don't meet a goal today, simply start again tomorrow. You're only human. Not only is life going to get in the way sometimes, but your own motivation and determination will lead you through ups and downs. One bad meal doesn't ruin a diet or fitness plan but using it as an excuse to give up absolutely will.

Accept that any setbacks you suffer are just part of the learning process. If your goal is important enough to you, you can pick yourself back up and begin where you left off.

If I Can Do it, Anyone Can

The last reminder I want to leave you with is that I should theoretically be the worst person in the world to be teaching you about focus and motivation. After all, my brain is literally working against me, trying to get me to bounce from one topic to another. And yet, I get paid to share my thoughts on the subject regularly. And now I've written a book on how to keep your mind on what matters.

The point is that if I can do it you certainly can. If you have an attention-deficit disorder you can follow my template and live a fun, engaging, and successful life. You can be productive and respected while bringing out the best in your personality. If you don't happen to have anything like that going on your brain then your path to the top will probably be easier.

I'm going to let you in on a little secret, one that I discovered a long time ago: there isn't any magic barrier preventing you from living the life you want. You can be wealthier, fitter, or more attractive. All it takes is the right focus and the kinds of habits that will lead you in a certain direction. The information you need to get six pack abs or a booming investment account is out there. You just need to absorb it and put it to use. No hidden force in the universe is going to notice you trying to succeed and sabotage the effort.

The plan I've outlined in this book has worked wonders for me. It hasn't just helped me to keep my mind from drifting from task to task, but also to pick up new skills and change my entire perspective on the way I live. My deepest hope is that they can do the same for you.

When I started this book I thought it was about me and what I had learned from living my life with ADHD. What I discovered in the process of putting my thoughts together, though, is that it's really about surviving – and thriving – in a world of distraction. It isn't about my journey, it's about yours.

By simply picking up a copy and committing the time to read it from cover to cover you have proven to me (and yourself) that you're serious about getting focused on what matters. Unfortunately, simply taking the time to look at the words I've laid out isn't going to be enough to actually create those changes. It's up to you to start putting these thoughts into action and developing new habits.

Are you ready to strip away the distractions that prevent you from finding the personal, academic, or professional success you've been searching for? I know you are, and I hope my ideas and experiences have helped to nudge you in the right direction. Now go do something amazing and be sure to tell me about it once you do!

The Magic of Decisions

I love what I do. I get to travel around the country (and sometimes the world), meet lots of interesting people, and see how a little bit of practical advice can completely change someone's life. It isn't just fun, it's gratifying on a lot of different levels.

However, there is a downside to my work. I've noticed over the years that when people leave one of my keynotes, workshops, or hypnosis shows, they are really pumped up to make some positive improvements. They may be so excited, in fact, that they tend to take on too many things at once.

I know I've been guilty of this in the past. I think we all have. There is a rush of motivation that comes with being exposed to new ideas and viewpoints that can lead us to think we are going to completely turn ourselves around in a new direction.

Remember the advice I've given you all along: treat focus as not just something that matters in the hour or two that's right in front of you, but also as you plot the course of the weeks, months, and years to come. See if you can zero in on the one or two changes you can make, starting today, that might make other improvements in your life easier.

Want an example? I often find that when things aren't going my way, the first thing I have to evaluate is my physical fitness. When my body isn't being treated well it affects my mind. That messes with my sleep, my concentration, and the routines I have put into place. I'm not saying one cheeseburger is going to ruin my life, I'm just letting you know that it's often the case that a "funk" I'm in can be traced back to a period where I had a crappy diet and skipped exercise.

For you, making that first change – right now when you're still excited about the possibilities – could involve getting more sleep, learning to make smarter to-do lists, or giving up a video game for a while. I can't set those priorities for you. What I can do is to give you the good advice to make sure those priorities are there in the first place. Otherwise, you might find yourself flailing in so many different ways that it's hard to stay on track. You can be motivated without being focused, but the results usually aren't that great.

Once you have decided what that first step looks like, go ahead and take it. Make a firm decision that your life is going to be different, even if it's just in one small way in the beginning. Write that goal down, tell your friends about it, and put up reminders everywhere. Make yourself accountable for it!

There is something truly powerful about making a decision and turning a corner. It's harder than considering what you might do someday or thinking about the possibilities. Once you actually stamp your intention into place, and make your intention public, you have a commitment that needs to be kept. For many people accountability is one of the biggest motivators. To not follow through would invite feelings of failure and possibly embarrassment.

Believe it or not, that's a good thing. You can use that. Change is almost always a little bit uncomfortable so you should confront that and own it from the beginning. It can drive you to keep going when you would rather give up. It's your secret weapon that forces you to put down the cheesesteak and pick up your running shoes. This is why a supportive friend, business coach, or mastermind group can be so valuable. They all help stay you on track

I'm not saying that you can just read this book and instantly fix every problem you have or take on every challenge that's in front of you. If you even skimmed the chapters, you already know that's not how I've built my life and career. There were a lot of failures and setbacks, but I learned from each one. Most importantly, I never really stopped (even if I did sort of trip or sit down for an extended rest every once in a while).

Make a decision about who and what you want to be and then put the first step of your plan into action. If it really matters to you then you'll find a way. Why you want to do something is always more important than how you'll do it.

I like to tell people magic isn't exactly fake. While it might be the case that I can't *really* make a dove disappear, it's also true that the hundreds of hours I spend practicing an illusion can bring an amazing idea to life. With enough hard work, I can bring the impossible to you right in front of your very eyes.

That's the power of hard work and it starts with a firm decision. Decide where your focus will take you and you'll be amazed at the way the world opens up and bends to your will. You have everything you need to turn yourself into a concentrated and motivated machine. Now go make it happen!

About the Author

Eric Mina is an author, hypnotist, and keynote speaker.

Learn more about him and his work at www.ericmina.com.

Made in the USA
Middletown, DE
25 August 2023

36928102R00083